D0780507

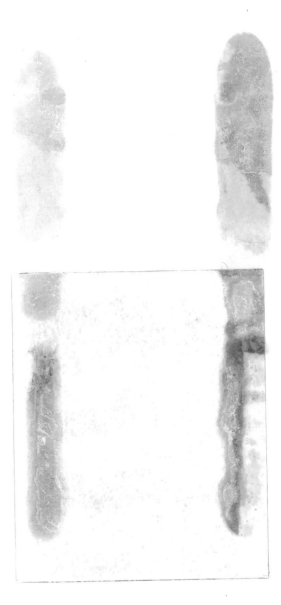

FIVE TEMPERAMENTS

Five Temperaments

ELIZABETH BISHOP   ROBERT LOWELL   JAMES MERRILL

ADRIENNE RICH   JOHN ASHBERY

DAVID KALSTONE

New York OXFORD UNIVERSITY PRESS 1977

PUBLIC LIBRARY SAN MATEO CALIFORNIA

Copyright © 1977 by David Kalstone
Library of Congress Catalogue Card Number: 76-42655

A list of credits appears on pp. 211-12,
which constitute an extension of this page.

Printed in the United States of America

78-00945

For Edmund White

CONTENTS

ACKNOWLEDGMENTS

This book owes a great deal to the example, the teaching and the generous spirit of the late Reuben Brower. I am grateful also to good friends for their indispensable critical advice: among them, Frank Bidart, Maxine Groffsky, Rachel Jacoff, Patrick Merla, Stephen Orgel, Richard Poirier and Edmund White. In James Raimes I have had the most patient and understanding of editors. Harry Ford has been kind to the project from the start. I want to thank the Research Council of Rutgers University and also the Hurst Professorship of Washington University under whose auspices I began this book.

Chapter 5 appeared in the *Denver Quarterly* (Winter 1976). A part of Chapter 1 appeared in *Ploughshares* (Vol. 2, No. 4, 1975).

FIVE TEMPERAMENTS

INTRODUCTION
Imagined Lives

Unreal, give back to us what once you gave
The imagination that we spurned and crave.

WALLACE STEVENS
"To the One of Fictive Music"

This is a book about the ways poets find to write about their lives. Or, more specifically, the ways some contemporary American poets have chosen to describe and dramatize their lives. Anyone who picks his way through the poetry magazines, the books and broadsheets, anyone who has tried to write a poem, knows firsthand the gap between urgency and achievement, between a felt need for self-disclosure and what stares back at the reader in black and white. Helen Vendler, reviewing the books of verse published in a single quarter of the year, begins by reminding herself:

> There is something of the letter, as Emily Dickinson and Thoreau knew, about every book sent out into a silent world. Reading the books of poetry published during one quarter of a given year is like opening the mailbox daily to a flood of letters, impassioned, reticent, wry, awkward, pompous, timid, arrogant, cheerful, touching, gifted, even stunning. . . . Sometimes, in the society of so many books, I feel pressed in on by too many voices, each, like the Ancient Mariner, with "strange power of speech," until I recall what a pitifully small fraction of all lived life is written down, how mutely most life goes to the grave. And then these poems seem precious shards, as Adrienne Rich once said in a poem, full of pathos—a fragment here, a glimpse there, a breath escaped from the tomb.[1]

Randall Jarrell, some twenty years earlier, facing a similar flood of books, took a more abrasive view:

> The good and mediocre books come in from week to week, and I put them aside and read them and think of what to say; but the "worthless" books come in day after day, like the cries and truck sounds from the street, and there is nothing that anyone could think of that is good enough for them. In the bad type of the thin pamphlets, in hand-set lines on imported paper, people's hard lives and hopeless ambitions have expressed themselves more directly and heartbreakingly than they have ever been expressed in any work of art: it is as if the writers had sent you their ripped-out arms and legs, with "This is a poem" scrawled on them in lipstick.[2]

During the years that have passed since Jarrell's essay a critic could easily become nostalgic about the security with which Jarrell identifies a "work of art." Many dismembered limbs seem on their way to becoming museum pieces. But the problem raised by both Vendler and Jarrell is always with us: how, when, if a poem passes, as through the eye of a needle, from need to accomplishment.

The question is raised in its severest form by the autobiographical impulses and elements in poetry—and so it is raised prominently by recent books in which American poets are writing more or less openly about themselves. It is important to ask—as with all writing about the self—in what ways the very act of writing poetry is a selective one. "If there were only," as Jarrell says, "some mechanism . . . for reasonably and systematically converting into poetry what we see and feel and are!"

But instead poems act as mysteriously as the pupil of the eye, narrowing and widening, allowing just enough light to help the writer see but not to bleach out the image. In this book I am interested in understanding what it is that poems admit of a poet's "autobiography," how much of it they can bear and handle. I have taken some soundings from the work of five very different American contemporaries, always bearing in mind the warning of one of them, John Ashbery, whose sense of his self-portrait is the most extreme and subversive of all:

> This otherness, this
> "Not-being-us" is all there is to look at
> In the mirror, though no one can say
> How it came to be this way. A ship
> Flying unknown colors has entered the harbor.[3]

There are no simple answers for such problems. But there are misleading ways to frame the question. A reviewer, himself a poet, is able to write, as late as 1976:

> There are two kinds of poets. The first believe that poetry is a language-skill, that poems are constructed with words, not emotions. Auden was of this opinion and said so more than once. . . . The other kind of poet believes that poetry is a product of feeling rather than wit. He believes that words are not chosen by the poet's rational mind but, to the contrary, may be forced upon him, and the best writing is done this way.[4]

The heart sinks at statements like this. They raise false and tired issues—as if one had to, or indeed could, choose between feeling and the medium expressing it. More than that, the critic writes as if the astonishing developments in American poetry of the past thirty years had not taken place. In career after career of poets who came of age after 1945, extraordinary energies have been combined and released. The period produced poets first recognized and praised for their formal excellence, who have since undergone radical transformations of style and subject matter. Robert Lowell is only the most obvious example—the perverse darling of a knotted metaphysical style who moved to the blunt revelations of *Life Studies*. Poets who were taught, like Yeats's school-children, to be neat in the best modern way have developed over several decades—sometimes through the efforts of seven or eight books of poems—highly individual compacts with the self. I am thinking of works like John Berryman's *Dream Songs*, Allen Ginsberg's *Kaddish*, Robert Lowell's *History*, John Ashbery's *Three Poems*, James Merrill's "The Book of Ephraim." How surprised many of these poets would have been early on to discover the course their writing lives would take: the dutiful early Adrienne Rich, for example, at Radcliffe and becoming a Yale Younger Poet, and who now gives vigorous expression to the anger, the dreams, the special voices of women, in some of the freer poetic forms devised by Pound and Williams and Olson.

Rich's career is a good example for another reason. Like many of the other poets I have mentioned, through all her changes she has kept in touch as well with her earlier poetic self, with its gifts, its limitations and resources, the rhythms now to be honored or challenged as the occasion demands. So, in "Meditations for a Savage Child," she expresses conflicting sympathies to a child baffled by efforts to socialize and civilize its instincts.

> In their own way, by their own lights
> they tried to care for you
> tried to teach you to care
> for objects of their caring
>
>   glossed oak planks, glass
>   whirled in a fire
>   to impossible thinness

An old and a new self are present here.[5] The divided typography makes clear what is already present in the poem's rhythms—indignation set against a residual attraction to familiar objects and the habit of cherishing.

Poets coming of age in the 1950s and early 1960s enjoyed what in retrospect is a peculiar combination of formalism and release. Let me oversimplify for a moment. A young man—less often a young woman—of the period wants to be a poet. He or she goes to college, and, though of course the young poet has secret childhood and adolescent favorites, at university much of his experience of other poetry is mediated for him. Writing poetry in those years became firmly yoked to the English literature curriculum in ways that it probably had not been in the past. Many of the young poets were taught to "read," and sometimes to write, by influential literary critics who were often poets themselves: John Crowe Ransom, Yvor Winters, Robert Penn Warren, R. P. Blackmur, Allen Tate. There were, for better or worse, English Studies, as there had not been in so narrow and disciplined a sense for the poetic giants of a generation earlier. Eliot, Pound, Stevens, Williams had, in a sense, forged their own literary criticism. A younger poet *studied* Eliot's essays. Or learned critical approaches to literature in English courses such as the ones Allen Ginsberg took under Lionel Trilling at Columbia, or James Merrill from Reuben Brower at Amherst. Brooks and Warren's *Understanding Poetry* taught students to be close readers of the Metaphysical poem. New Criticism brought them up to think in terms of the single "perfect" poem. One could not expect to encounter much, if any, contemporary verse in the classroom. Trained to be the ideal reader of Donne or Marvell, a young student had to seek out modern poems in the literary quarterlies or come upon them through the chance recommendations of informed friends and teachers. It was largely a private affair. And whether a beginning poet fell under the influence of Eliot's ironic elegies or Stevens's high rhapsodies or William Carlos Williams's homemade documentaries, he was prepared to think of a poem as something "other," something objective, free of the quirks of the personal.

That was one side of the picture. The other side, equally important, was the way those same young poets reacted to (*to*, rather than *against*) their training. Richard Howard, in a happy phrase, calls this postwar generation of poets "the children of Midas." He is thinking of the last phases of the myth, when King Midas, having discovered that *everything* he touches ("his food, his women, his words") inconveniently turns to gold, prays to lose the gift of the golden touch. "What seems to me especially proper to these poets," Howard tells us, ". . . is the last development, the longing to *lose* the gift of order, despoiling the self of all that had been, merely, *propriety*."[6] There were some very extreme examples, of course: the Ginsberg of *Howl*, the Plath of *Ariel*. And it is a very special mark of this period that a poet as bookish, as literary, as "academic" as John Berryman should also have written one of the wildest and most disquieting autobiographical poems of his time.

Most important in the long run was the new ease and pluralism in American poetry, a changing notion of what a poet was and did. Before the 1960s there had been relatively few poetry readings. A reading was something given by THE poet—Eliot, Auden, Stevens, Frost, Thomas—a demonstration of the arias the audience already knew and wanted to hear from the famous lips, rather than a chance to get acquainted—which has become more and more the case—with a new or different voice. American poetry in the 1960s seemed to be taking over some of the traditional functions and tones of fiction (especially the short story); it seemed more personal and explosive than it had been in the 1950s, more dedicated to self-disclosure.

The colloquial range and inclusiveness of a poet such as Frank O'Hara was almost unprecedented—his breezy connections between the streets of New York and the world of the French surrealists, his independence of the formal traditions of English poetry and even of the style of modernism represented by Pound and Eliot. Many poets learned from what John Ashbery praised as O'Hara's "big, airy structures unlike anything previous in American poetry and indeed unlike poetry, more like the inspired ramblings of a mind open to the point of distraction."[7]

There were books of poems which, because of their subject matter—insanity, divorce, sex, alcoholism—gained notoriety beyond the select band which read verse: W. D. Snodgrass's *Heart's Needle*, Robert Lowell's *Life Studies*, Anne Sexton's *To Bedlam and Part Way Back*. Critics talked about "confessional" poetry, a convenient but misleading label. The fact is that American poetry of this period became increasingly available to autobiographical energies of *all* sorts, not simply to writing which was desperate and on the edge. It is easiest to notice this development in the crisis mentality of "confessional" poems, and certainly their explicitness had a challenging effect on poets of every degree of frankness or reticence. Over a twenty-year period, in the sheer variety, versatility and openness of postwar American poetry, individual poets have traced curves of personal growth and change, of courtships, marriages and divorce, of an emerging awareness of the needs and angers felt by women, of the particular terms of sexuality felt between men and women, men and men, women and women.

But we need not confuse the excitement of new subject matter with the special nature of these writings as *poems*. One objection to the term "confessional" is that it overstresses the notion of the poem as an instant communication (and the poet as an instant communicant). Richard Poirier, writing about novels, warns against the "tendency to treat experiences in fiction as if somehow they existed independently of the style which creates them and which creates, too, the environment in which these experiences make or do not make sense."[8] A poem is itself an act, part of the life it "describes." The environment that style creates is, in recent poetry, often one of struggle, improvisation and resistance, as vital as the raw data—city, weather, mother's maiden name, father's death, school-day humiliations—which make the poem seem familiar and more obviously autobiographical.

To trace out these inner landscapes takes a steady, long-range habit of attention—like listening for the obsessive patterns, the repeated words and phrases that finally bring experiences into focus, in a language one does not yet perfectly know. Poetry has always made such demands on its committed readers. But, complicating that, contemporary poets are seeing their work in larger or more provisional units: long poems, sequences, mixtures of poetry and prose, or flowing self-revising units such as Lowell's separate editions of *Notebook*, Rich's *Leaflets*, or A. R. Ammons's *Tape for the Turn of the Year*. There is less concern for writing the single "perfect" poem. Readers interested in a poet's development, are learning to recognize the slow accumulation of autobiography in successive collections of lyric poems.

In a period so various—and one in which poets draw with such improvisatory pleasure on a number of traditions—generalizations are almost beside the point. What I hope to do in this book is to follow the work of five poets with developed careers. I have preferred to talk about a few poets and to talk about them in detail—the only way to trace the emerging strength of a writer and to learn how he or she finds a voice and a writing self. I do not concentrate on wonderful single poems for their own sake—though the poets I discuss here have written them. Nor am I concerned with excellent miscellaneous collections of a poet's verse. The focus is on the *growth* of the work. I discuss poets who have published enough so that their writing is felt as an ongoing activity. Above all, I have chosen poets who have given me a strong and developing sense of how poetry can serve as autobiography, who have helped me understand the revisions of the self that come through writing verse: how this happens, its resources, its limits.

I have also chosen with an eye to contrast. The poets are radically different from one another. Though my chapters stand as separate readings, they also point comparisons which allow one poet to reflect, by implication, upon the work of another. No selection for this sort of book could be fully representative or satisfy all readers. Instead of attempting coverage, I have kept to my subject and, of course, I have written about poets I admire. They give a sense of the varying possibilities of writing about the self, and each poses a quite separate critical problem.

Elizabeth Bishop, who opens the book, is on the surface of things the most reticent of the writers, the one readers will be most surprised to find here, the one most linked to the "impersonal" writing of the previous generation. What I have felt most moving about her work is her slowly emerging, careful acknowledgment of the autobiographical strength of her poems. Adrienne Rich is a more obvious choice for a book of this sort, the one poet among the five whose belief in the autobiographical force of a poem rises virtually to a political statement. I have juxtaposed Robert Lowell and James Merrill in two central chapters (which might have been a unit called "Life Studies") partly because these poets are hardly ever mentioned in the same breath, and because they provide the most energetically opposed uses of the resources of the past—and particularly of childhood—that we have among our contemporaries. I close the book with a chapter on John Ashbery because he offers at one and the same time the most desperate examples of attempts to capture the privacy of minute feelings and the most penetrating critiques of that impulse.

Ashbery was to say of the childhood memories in "The Skaters" that "I didn't want them to be specific ones that applied to me but only ones that anybody would use if they were thinking autobiographically; they were just to be forms of autobiography. . . ."[9] It is the "forms of autobiography" that are my subject—some recent and contrasting examples of how individuality or temperament emerges as poetic form. I intend the word "temperament," of course, in its nonpejorative sense, as Wallace Stevens used it when he remarked that, "Temperament is a more explicit word than personality and would no doubt be the exact word to use, since it emphasizes the manner of thinking and feeling." Stevens, one of the least overtly autobiographical of poets, understood exactly what part the personal played: "It is often said of a man that his work is autobiographical in spite of every subterfuge. It cannot be otherwise . . . even though it may be totally without reference to himself."[10] I have kept that paradox in front of me in writing this book.

I ELIZABETH BISHOP
Questions of Memory, Questions of Travel

Elizabeth Bishop, to her credit, has always been hard to "place." In the surveys of American poetry she is not linked to any particular school. She has had, from the very start, her share of prizes and praise; her work is admired by many poets who do not admire one another. Though on occasion she has had the grants and university positions which keep poets alive in America, she only rarely gives the public readings which keep poets visible. She has lived abroad for long stretches of her life, most recently in Brazil. Her books of poems, eagerly awaited, appear infrequently: *North & South* (1946); *A Cold Spring* (1955); *Questions of Travel* (1965); *The Complete Poems* (1969); *Geography III* (1976).

Bishop is probably the most honored yet most elusive of contemporary poets. Who else, with some of her best poems still to be written, would have entitled a volume *The Complete Poems*? She was, until very recently, "read unreasonably little and praised reasonably much," as Randall Jarrell said of Marianne Moore. There are many reasons for this, but the ones which interest me here have to do with the accidents of critical attention. Bishop's first book was so individual and striking that certain pieces from *North & South*—poems like "The Fish" and "The Man-Moth"— have been reprinted over and over in anthologies. She has become known as the author of single stunning poems, fewer from the later volumes than from the earlier. Wonderful as the anthologized poems may be, they give, even for anthologies, an unusually stunted version of Bishop's variety, of the way her writing has emerged, of her developing concerns.

There is a second problem: the deceptively simple surface of Bishop's work. Critics have praised her descriptive powers and treated her as something of a miniaturist. As mistakenly as with the work of Marianne Moore, they have sometimes asked if Bishop's is poetry at all. Bishop's early poems show a deep affinity with Marianne Moore's exact observant style: "An appropriately selected foundation for Miss Bishop's work," said Randall Jarrell. But he was also quick to see Bishop as "less driven into desperate straits or dens of innocence, and taking this Century of Polycarp more for granted."[1] Jarrell is one of those critics who urges us to look for the inner landscape and not to treat a poet's descriptive powers as if they were ends in themselves, or a weaker form of expression. He was able to show Moore's accuracy and understatement to be an instrument of ironic self-protectiveness. ("Her Shield" is the title of his essay.) By implication, he teaches us to ask similar questions about Bishop. Unlike the relatively armored approach of Marianne Moore, Bishop's precise explorations become a way of countering and encountering a lost world. Merely to praise her "famous eye" would be a way of avoiding larger issues. We need to know what is seen, and how the eye, with what Kenneth Burke calls its "disguised rituals," initiates us into human fears and wishes.

1

Robert Lowell, thinking back to the time before he wrote *Life Studies*, felt that Bishop's work "seemed to belong to a later century."[2] It wasn't so much a matter of experimental forms. In *North & South* (1946) there were a number of emblematic poems—"The Map," "The Monument," "The Gentleman of Shalott" among them—some in formal stanzas, some strictly rhymed. Still, from

the very start, there was something about her work for which ele-
gantly standard literary analysis was not prepared. Readers have
been puzzled, as when one critic writes about "Florida": "the
poet's exuberance provides a scattering of images whose relevance
to the total structure is open to question. It is as though Miss
Bishop stopped along the road home to examine every buttercup
and asphodel she saw."[3] First of all, Bishop writes about alligators,
mangrove swamps, skeletons and shells—things exotic and wild,
not prettified. More important, there is some notion of neat and
total structure which the critic expects and imposes, but which
the poem subverts. What makes the quoted critic nervous is a
quality which becomes more and more prominent in Bishop's
work—her apparent lack of insistence on meanings beyond the
surface of the poem, the poem's seeming randomness and disintegration. There is something personal, even quirky, about her apparently straightforward descriptive poems which, on early readings, it is hard to identify. This is an offhand way of speaking
which Bishop has come to trust and master, especially in her important book of 1965, *Questions of Travel*, and in the extraordinary
poems she has published since then.

I am talking about matters of tone, the kind of authority a
single voice will claim over the material included in a poem. Anyone who has heard Miss Bishop read will know how flat and modest
her voice is, how devoid of flourish, how briefly she holds her final
chords and cadences and allows a poem to resonate. Here is the
beginning of "In the Waiting Room":

> In Worcester, Massachusetts,
> I went with Aunt Consuelo
> to keep her dentist's appointment
> and sat and waited for her
> in the dentist's waiting room.

Or another opening ("Filling Station"):

> Oh, but it is dirty!
> —this little filling station,
> oil-soaked, oil-permeated

to a disturbing, over-all
black translucency.
Be careful with that match!

And this is the end of "The Bight":

Click. Click. Goes the dredge,
and brings up a dripping jawful of marl.
All the untidy activity continues,
awful but cheerful.

I have chosen the plainest and most provocative examples of the apparently random in order to raise questions common to much poetry after Wallace Stevens: how is meaning developed from individual and unamplified details? How does the observer's apparent lack of insistence, devoid of rhetorical pressure, rise to significance (if, indeed, that is the word for it)? Howard Nemerov gives us one answer: "Vision begins with a fault in this world's smooth façade."[4] But Bishop finds that fault, that break from observation into the unknown, almost impossible to locate. "There is no split," she remarks in a letter:

Dreams, works of art (some) glimpses of the always-more-successful surrealism of everyday life, unexpected moments of empathy (is it?), catch a peripheral vision of whatever it is one can never really see full-face but that seems enormously important. I can't believe we are wholly irrational—and I do admire Darwin—But reading Darwin one admires the beautiful solid case being built up out of his endless, heroic observations, almost unconscious or automatic—and then comes a sudden relaxation, a forgetful phrase, and one feels that strangeness of his undertaking, sees the lonely young man, his eye fixed on facts and minute details, sinking or sliding giddily off into the unknown. What one seems to want in art, in experiencing it, is the same thing that is necessary for its creation, a self-forgetful, perfectly useless concentration.[5]

Heroic observation; eyes fixed on facts and minute details, sinking, sliding giddily off into the unknown; a self-forgetful, perfectly useless concentration. What she sees in Darwin, we can see in her own efforts. Take "Florida" (the poem our critic found disorganized)—a poem of almost Darwinian concentration.

The opening line is so disarming, almost trivializing, that we are in danger of taking what follows for granted: the odd changes of scale that are among this poem's secrets.

> The state with the prettiest name,
> the state that floats in brackish water,
> held together by mangrove roots
> that bear while living oysters in clusters,
> and when dead strew white swamps with skeletons,
> dotted as if bombarded, with green hummocks
> like ancient cannon-balls sprouting grass.

The scale changes as rapidly as Gulliver's: first the whole state, afloat, intact with its boundaries, the mapmaker's or aerial photographer's vision; then an organism (held together by mangrove roots), the geologist's or botanist's fanciful X ray. Her Florida is a barnacled world refined to residues. Oysters dot the mangrove roots; dead mangroves strew the swamps with skeletons. Dead turtles leave their skulls and their shells, which are themselves hosts to other growths, barnacled. The coastline is looped with seashells painstakingly and exotically named. There is sediment in the water; solvents in wood-smoke; charring on stumps and dead trees. Yet the charring is "like black velvet." The residues studding this landscape are its principal ornaments as well: artistic and historical growths, like the "tide-looped strings of fading shells" turning the "monotonous . . . sagging coast-line" to something else.

At first the description occurs in a free-floating eternal present, a series of phrases which don't commit the observer to any main verb at all. They seem if anything to exclude her, re-awakening memories of geological change that stretch far before and beyond her in scale, habitually repeated historical action. The strange shifts of scale—of size and space—in a seemingly timeless, self-renewing present remind us constantly, by implication, of the frailty of our merely human observer. A descriptive poem, which in other hands, say Whitman's, appropriates landscapes and objects, here makes us aware just how, just why we are excluded from such appropriations.

Only when we get to the buzzards, two-thirds of the way through the poem, is there a form of the present tense (they "are drifting down, down, down") restricted to her particular moment of watching, a definite *now*. Here also, two strange mirrors in which we do not find ourselves. First:

> Thirty or more buzzards are drifting down, down, down,
> over something they have spotted in the swamp,
> in circles like stirred-up flakes of sediment
> sinking through water.
> Smoke from woods-fires filters fine blue solvents.

And then:

> After dark, the fireflies map the heavens in the marsh
> until the moon rises.

The four elements form a self-enclosed world. Creatures of the air mirror the earth's discards (are they really there?) floating through water; and fire, as if completing the cycle, exhales fine smoke into the blue. Then again with the fireflies, air and flickering fire are reflected in the marsh, earth and water together. In other words, alternate creations dwarf or frame the poet's own: the long scale of eroding nature with its fossils and predators (buzzards, mosquitoes with "ferocious obbligatos"), and then the daily repeating creations and fadings. When the moon comes up, the landscape pales. Its wonderful sounds and colors—the flashy tanagers, the pelicans gold-winged at sunset, the musical screeching—turn skeletal once more.

The world in its processes provides a delicate model for the poet's work, for art—its shells with beautiful names, its finely observed (and alliterative) oysters in clusters. But the poem continually stresses how such contrivance is made for fading and how nature's contrivances survive the artist's own. Building toward a phrase whose effect is worthy of what she admires in Darwin ("a sudden relaxation, a forgetful phrase"), Bishop sums up the impact of the scene, grasped for the fullness of her own understanding:

> Cold white, not bright, the moonlight is coarse-meshed,
> and the careless, corrupt state is all black specks
> too far apart, and ugly whites; the poorest
> post-card of itself.

At the end Florida contracts to the alligator's five primitive calls ("friendliness, love, mating, war, and a warning"), and with its whimper is restored to darkness and its mysterious identity as "the Indian Princess."

Bishop exposes us to a more ambitious version of her almost toneless observer in a poem which reaches back to her Nova Scotia childhood, "At the Fishhouses." Here is the opening:

> Although it is a cold evening,
> down by one of the fishhouses
> an old man sits netting,
> his net, in the gloaming almost invisible
> a dark purple-brown,
> and his shuttle worn and polished.
> The air smells so strong of codfish
> it makes one's nose run and one's eyes water.
> The five fishhouses have steeply peaked roofs
> and narrow, cleated gangplanks slant up
> to storerooms in the gables
> for the wheelbarrows to be pushed up and down on.
> All is silver: the heavy surface of the sea,
> swelling slowly as if considering spilling over,
> is opaque, but the silver of the benches,
> the lobster pots, and masts, scattered
> among the wild jagged rocks,
> is of an apparent translucence
> like the small old buildings with an emerald moss
> growing on their shoreward walls.
> The big fish tubs are completely lined
> with layers of beautiful herring scales
> and the wheelbarrows are similarly plastered
> with creamy iridescent coats of mail,
> with small iridescent flies crawling on them.

At first, as in "Florida," a landscape seems almost without a spectator, the speaker comically unwelcome in an air which smacks of another element and which makes her eyes water and her nose run. She slowly exposes the scene, present tense, with a tempered willingness to let it speak for itself in declarative simplicity. Things *are*; things *have*. The lone fisherman, a Wordsworthian solitary, is worn into the scene, his net "almost invisible," his shuttle "worn and polished," his "black old knife" with a blade "almost worn away." The dense opening description—deliberately slow, close to fifty lines of the poem—is in all details of sight, sense and sound intended to subject us to the landscape, to draw us deeply into it. "The five fishhouses have steeply peaked roofs / and narrow, cleated gangplanks slant up": even the clotted consonants and doubling of adjectives force these words apart and force us to dwell on them, as if to carve out some certainty of vision. The reader is meant to become what the speaker jokingly claims herself to be later in this poem: "a believer in total immersion."

From this immersion a pattern gathers, unhurried but persistent: present, for example, in the odd half-rhyme of *codfish* and *polished*, or in the unassuming repetition of *iridescent*. The wheelbarrows are "plastered / with creamy iridescent coats of mail, / with small iridescent flies crawling on them." The crudeness and the delicacy of these details are made to appear strokes of the same master, of the landscape's age-old subjection to the sea, to the caking, the plastering, the lining, the silvering-over which turns everything to iridescence or sequins, as at the same time it rusts them and wears them away.

In its fidelity to setting—to what is both jagged and strangely jewelled—the poem accumulates the sense of an artistry beyond the human, one that stretches over time, chiselling and decorating with its strange erosions. The human enterprise depends upon and is dwarfed by the sea, just as the fishhouse ramps lead out of, but back into the water: "Down at the water's edge, at the place / where they haul up the boats, up the long ramp / descending into the water." Precisely by imagining these encircling powers, the speaker wins some authority over them. This is her largest gesture, reflected in some smaller moments of propitiation: offering a cigarette to the fisherman, and with odd simplicity singing Baptist hymns to a moderately curious seal, true creature of that "element bearable to no mortal." Behind them—or more to the point "behind us"—as if left behind in merely human history "a million Christmas trees stand / waiting for Christmas."

This "believer in total immersion," through her patient wooing or conjuring, finally wins a certain elevation of tone, a vision, in a twice-repeated phrase, of the sea "Cold dark deep and absolutely clear."

>   . . . The water seems suspended
> above the rounded gray and blue-gray stones.
> I have seen it over and over, the same sea, the same,
> slightly, indifferently swinging above the stones,
> icily free above the stones,
> above the stones and then the world.
> If you should dip your hand in,
> your wrist would ache immediately,
> your bones would begin to ache and your hand would burn
> as if the water were a transmutation of fire
> that feeds on stones and burns with a dark gray flame.
> If you tasted it, it would first taste bitter,
> then briny, then surely burn your tongue.
> It is like what we imagine knowledge to be:
> dark, salt, clear, moving, utterly free,
> drawn from the cold hard mouth
> of the world, derived from the rocky breasts
> forever, flowing and drawn, and since
> our knowledge is historical, flowing, and flown.

The poet returns knowledge to concreteness, as if breaking it down into its elements (dark, salt, clear). The speaker herself seems drawn into the elements: at first jokingly in the fishy air which makes the nose run, the eyes water; then in the burning if one dips one's hands, as if water were a "transmutation of fire that feeds on stones." The absorbing and magical transformations of earth, air, fire and water into one another (as in "Florida") make it impossible—and unnecessary—to distinguish *knowledge* from the *sea*, to determine what, grammatically, is "derived from the rocky breasts / forever." With a final fluency she leaves her declarative descriptions behind and captures a rhythm at once mysterious and acknowledging limitations ("flowing and drawn . . . flowing and flown").

"At the Fishhouses" makes explicit what is usually implicit, invisible and vital in Miss Bishop's poems, like a pulse: a sense of the encircling and eroding powers in whose presence all minute observations are valuably made. She is, in fact, rather like a sandpiper she describes in another poem: the bird pictured as subject to the water's roar, the earth's shaking—imagined in "a state of controlled panic, a student of Blake." He watches the sand, no detail too small ("Sandpiper"):

> The world is a mist. And then the world is
> minute and vast and clear. The tide
> is higher or lower. He couldn't tell you which.
> His beak is focussed; he is preoccupied,
>
> looking for something, something, something.
> Poor bird, he is obsessed!
> The millions of grains are black, white, tan, and gray,
> mixed with quartz grains, rose and amethyst.

Here again are those shifts of scale which, instead of unsettling, actually strengthen our perspective. The poem is a critique of Blake's auguries of innocence: his seeing the world in a grain of sand. "The world is a mist. And then the world is / minute and vast and clear." The adjectives appear to make a quiet claim. Yet what an odd collocation—minute and vast and clear. The scales are not really commensurable; one sees the world, one sees the grain of sand, and the clarity comes in making a primitive and definite distinction about what is and is not within our grasp. The bird, on the one hand, is battered and baffled by the waves, the misty "sheets of interrupting water"; on the other hand it attends and stares, is preoccupied, obsessed with the grains of sand, a litany of whose colors, minutely and beautifully distinguished, ends the poem. That is all it knows of the world.

These poems both describe and set themselves at the limits of description. Bishop lets us know that every detail is a boundary, not a Blakean microcosm. Because of the limits they suggest, details vibrate with a meaning beyond mere physical presence. Landscapes meant to sound detached are really inner landscapes. They show an effort at reconstituting the world as if it were in danger of being continually lost. It is only this sense of *precarious* possession that accounts for the way Bishop looks at the city waking up ("Love Lies Sleeping"):

> From the window I see
>
> an immense city, carefully revealed,
> made delicate by over-workmanship,
>   detail upon detail,
>   cornice upon façade,
>
> reaching so languidly up into
> a weak white sky, it seems to waver there.
>   (where it has slowly grown
>   in skies of water-glass
>
> from fused beads of iron and copper crystals,
> the little chemical "garden" in a jar
>   trembles and stands again,
>   pale blue, blue-green, and brick.)

That human contrivance is frail and provisional is clear not only from the "wavering" but also from the odd, habitual changes of scale: an immense city, carefully revealed, is also a little chemical garden in a jar. That it should be seen as workmanship at all is a miracle of freshness, a confusion of proportions, part aerial vision, part closeup as of some miraculous insect civilization. Bishop triumphs in the surprising coincidence of mechanics and natural growth, fused beads of crystal, a little chemical garden—a balancing act to portray our fragile ingenuity.

The ability to see such accomplishments as provisional explains the power of one of Bishop's apparently random poems, "The Bight." It is subtitled "on my birthday," the only suggestion of much resonance beyond the impression of a tide-battered inlet— muddy at low tide, with dredges, pelicans, marl, sponge boats, sharktails hung up to dry, boats beached, some wrecked. What animates the scene this time is the observer's deliberate activity, celebrating her birthday in an off-key way with an unrelenting and occasionally mischievous series of comparisons: pilings dry as matches; water turning to gas (and which Baudelaire might hear turning to marimba music); pelicans crashing like pickaxes; man-of-war birds opening tails like scissors; sharktails hanging like plow-shares. The whole rundown world is domesticated by comparisons to our mechanical contrivances, our instruments of workaday survival, enabling, in turn, an outrageous simile (stove-boats "like torn-open, unanswered letters") and an equally outrageous pun ("The bight is littered with old correspondences"). The letters wickedly enough bring Baudelaire back into the poem, merge with his "correspondences." They are unanswered letters to boot, in a poem where the author has shot off one comparison after another, like firecrackers. No wonder then that a dredge at the end perfectly accompanies this poet's activities:

> Click. Click. Goes the dredge,
> and brings up a dripping jawful of marl.
> All the untidy activity continues,
> awful but cheerful.

This is what she allows for her birthday: the pointed celebration of small-craft victories in a storm-ridden inlet.

It is no accident that much of Bishop's work is carried on at the mercy of or in the wake of the tides. There are divided and distinguished stages in her encounters: moments of civilized, provisional triumph; and then again, times when landscapes leave us behind— the northern seas of "At the Fishhouses," the abundant decay of "Florida" and later, of her adopted Brazil, magnetic poles sensed even in the title of her first volume, *North & South*. Our mortal temperate zones seem in some ways the excluded middle where we possess a language of precarious, even doomed distinctions.

2

The fact that Bishop sought worlds which dwarf us, landscapes from which we are excluded, is best glossed by a wonderful and very important story, "In the Village." The tale reaches back to a Nova Scotia childhood, a version of her own. Her mother was taken to a sanitarium when Bishop was five; she never saw her again. The story is told through the child's eyes. In one scene the young girl watches her mother, who is just back from a sanitarium and coming out of two years of mourning, being fitted for a new dress. "The dressmaker was crawling around and around on her knees eating pins as Nebuchadnezzar had crawled eating grass." The child stands in the doorway.

> Clang.
> *Clang.*
> Oh, beautiful sounds, from the blacksmith's shop at the end of the garden! Its gray roof, with patches of moss, could be seen above the lilac bushes. Nate was there—Nate, wearing a long black leather apron over his trousers and bare chest, sweating hard, a black leather cap on top of dry, thick, black-and-gray curls, a black sooty face; iron filings, whiskers, and gold teeth, all together, and a smell of red-hot metal and horses' hoofs.
> *Clang.*
> The pure note: pure and angelic.
> The dress was all wrong. She screamed.
> The child vanishes.[6]

The child vanishes literally, and metaphorically as well, in that moment of awakening and awareness of inexplicable adult pain. From this point on the story is told in the first person and in the present tense, as if she had been jolted into reclaiming something first seen as a distant tableau and dream. Memories of the mother's scream echo through scenes which are also, as in the pungent energy of the blacksmith shop, rich strong recollections of life in a Nova Scotia village. At the end, the mother gone for good, the threats and village harmonies come together for the last time.

> Every Monday afternoon I go past the blacksmith's shop with the package under my arm, hiding the address of the sanitarium with my arm and my other hand.
>
> Going over the bridge, I stop and stare down into the river. All the little trout that have been too smart to get caught—for how long now?—are there, rushing in flank movements, foolish assaults and retreats, against and away from the old sunken fender of Malcolm McNeil's Ford. It has lain there for ages and is supposed to be a disgrace to us all. So are the tin cans that glint there, brown and gold.
>
> From above, the trout look as transparent as the water, but if one did catch one, it would be opaque enough, with a little slick moon-white belly with a pair of tiny, pleated, rose-pink fins on it. The leaning willows soak their narrow yellowed leaves.
>
> Clang.
>
> *Clang.*
>
> Nate is shaping a horseshoe.
>
> Oh, beautiful pure sound!
>
> It turns everything else to silence.
>
> But still, once in a while, the river gives an unexpected gurgle. "*Slp*," it says, out of glassy-ridged brown knots sliding along the surface.
>
> *Clang.*
>
> And everything except the river holds its breath.
>
> Now there is no scream. Once there was one and it settled slowly down to earth one hot summer afternoon; or did it float up, into that dark, too dark, blue sky? But surely it has gone away, forever.
>
> *Clang.*
>
> It sounds like a bell buoy out at sea.
>
> It is the elements speaking: earth, air, fire, water.
>
> All those other things—clothes, crumbling postcards, broken china; things damaged and lost, sickened or destroyed; even the frail almost-lost scream—are they too frail for us to hear their voices long, too mortal?
>
> Nate!
>
> Oh, beautiful sound, strike again![7]

What sounds like a bell buoy out at sea? The scream? The blacksmith's anvil? The two finally merging? "In the Village" is the vital center from which many of Bishop's poems radiate, the darker side of their serene need to reclaim "the elements speaking: earth, air, fire, water." She printed it among the poems of her 1965 volume, *Questions of Travel*, as if to make that point.

For a moment "In the Village" offers a radiant primal world, available to human energies. It is almost unique in Bishop's work for the way it resolves tensions between the remembered, inaccessible, inhuman call of the four elements and her affectionate grasp of the more precarious details of human life. In the glow of memory she is for once licensed to glide from the scream ("But surely it has gone away, forever") to the noise of the anvil, the two distantly merged like the bell buoy at sea, the elements speaking. For once, in the suffused light of childhood, she is allowed to hear those perfectly inhuman elements as if they were the voices of paradise, a fulfilled retreat from the intense inescapable world of change and loss. For once, losing hold of details is not an engulfment or a drowning, but a situation quietly accepted with a muted question:

> All those other things—clothes, crumbling postcards, broken china; things damaged and lost, sickened or destroyed; even the frail almost-lost scream—are they too frail for us to hear their voices long, too mortal?

No wonder then that Bishop was drawn again and again to her Northern and tropical landscapes whose scale and temperature are so different from our own. Exile and travel are at the heart of her poems from the very start—and sometimes as if they could reconstitute the vision of "In the Village," as if they led somewhere, a true counter to loss. Bishop is spellbound by the polar world in an early poem, "The Imaginary Iceberg." "Self-made from elements least visible," the iceberg "saves itself perpetually and adorns / only itself." Of that tempting self-enclosed world, a frosty palace of art, she writes, "We'd rather have the iceberg than the ship, / although it meant the end of travel." This is, in an idiom fraught with danger, "a scene a sailor'd give his eyes for."

Again, in the wonderful "Over 2000 Illustrations and a Complete Concordance," a traveller is tantalized by the promise of vision beyond the random encounter. Childhood memories of etchings of the Holy Land in an old Bible make her yearn for something beyond the *and* and *and* of pointlessly accumulated travel. This is the end of the poem:

> Everything only connected by "and" and "and."
> Open the book. (The gilt rubs off the edges
> of the pages and pollinates the fingertips.)
> Open the heavy book. Why couldn't we have seen
> this old Nativity while we were at it?
> —the dark ajar, the rocks breaking with light,
> an undisturbed, unbreathing flame,
> colorless, sparkless, freely fed on straw,
> and, lulled within, a family with pets,
> —and looked and looked our infant sight away.

Like the "scene a sailor'd give his eyes for," that last phrase ("looked and looked our infant sight away") carries a mysterious yearning to stop observing, which it also guards against. Bishop never entirely gives in. She glimpses the terrifying folk truth behind the apparent satisfactions of a sight "we'd give our eyes for." And if we are to see the old Nativity in "Over 2000 Illustrations," if the memory of engravings in a beloved childhood book allows us once more to trust experience as sacramental, if such travel will reconstitute the blasted family of "In the Village" (the poem envisions rocks breaking with light "and lulled within a family with pets"), then what will it mean to "look and look our infant sight away"? Where or when is *away*? Is it a measureless absorption in the scene? Or, on the contrary, a loss of powers, as in "to waste away"? Or a welcome relinquishment, to be gathered back into the world of childhood, to return to "infant" sight—it keeps its Latin root, "speechless."

Bishop, sensing dangers, only hints at satisfaction. "Over 2000

Illustrations and a Complete Concordance" is almost a farewell to such temptations. There are in her poems no final visions. She moves away from "We'd rather have the iceberg than the ship, / although it meant the end of travel" to the "Questions of Travel" entertained in her third book. There, in tones more relaxed than ever before, she learns to trust the saving, continuous, precise pursuits of the exile's eye.

3

The volume *Questions of Travel* in effect constitutes a sequence of poems, its Brazilian landscapes not so much providing answers as initiating us into the mysteries of how questions are asked. It is important that the book also includes poems about her Nova Scotia childhood and the central story of that period, "In the Village." In the light of those memories, the Brazilian poems become a model of how, with difficulty and pleasure, pain and precision, we re-introduce ourselves into a world.

There are three important initiating poems: in order, "Arrival at Santos," "Brazil, January 1, 1502" and "Questions of Travel." The first is deliberately superficial, comic, sociable. We watch her straining from tourist into traveller, after the disappointments of Santos, which like all ports is like soap or postage stamps—necessary but, "wasting away like the former, slipping the way the latter / do when we mail the letters we wrote on the boat." The familiar and merely instrumental melt away and we know something more than geographical is meant by the last line: "We are driving to the interior."

We go there by means of one of Bishop's characteristic changes of scale. "Arrival at Santos"—it's not Bishop's usual practice—had been dated at the end, *January, 1952*. The next poem is "Brazil, January 1, 1502," and its first word is the generalizing *Januaries*. No longer in the "here" and "now" of the uninstructed tourist, the poem fans out into the repeating present of the botanist and the anthropologist. Our drive to the interior is through the looking glass of natural history. There is a comforting epigraph from Lord

Clark's *Landscape into Art*, "embroidered nature . . . tapestried landscape," that seems to familiarize the scene, appropriate it for European sensibilities. Yet this is a wild burgeoning tapestry, not "filled in" with foliage but "every square inch *filling in* with foliage," tirelessly self-renewing. Its distinctions of shade and color force her into relentless unflagging specificity: "big leaves, little leaves, and giant leaves, / blue, blue-green, and olive." A parade of shades: silver-gray, rust red, greenish white, blue-white. The powers of description are deliberately and delightfully taxed; it's hard for mere humans to keep up.

Then, with a bow to our desire for a familiar tapestry, Bishop draws our attention to something in the foreground. It is first identified as "Sin: / five sooty dragons near some massy rocks." The rocks are "worked with lichens" and "threatened from underneath by moss / in lovely hell-green flames." Then, in a deliberate change of scale, the little morality play turns to something wilder, more riveting, making fun of our tame exaggerations. Those dragons are, in fact, lizards in heat.

> The lizards scarcely breathe; all eyes
> are on the smaller, female one, back-to,
> her wicked tail straight up and over,
> red as red-hot wire.

Then the most daring change of all:

> Just so the Christians, hard as nails,
> tiny as nails, and glinting,
> in creaking armor, came and found it all,
> not unfamiliar.

For a moment, until we unravel the syntax, "just so" identifies the invaders with the lizards in heat. Tiny in scale, dwarfed by the scene, the settlers, after Mass, are out hunting Indian women:

> they ripped away into the hanging fabric,
> each out to catch an Indian for himself—
> those maddening little women who kept calling,
> calling to each other (or had the birds waked up?)
> and retreating, always retreating, behind it.

The tapestry—initially it seemed like a device to domesticate the landscape—instead excludes invaders from it. At the beginning we were identified with those settlers of 1502: "Nature greets our eyes / exactly as she must have greeted theirs." At the end that proves to be a dubious privilege. Nature's tapestry endures, renews itself. After our initial glimpse of order, we shrink like Alice or Gulliver—toy intruders, marvelling.

Bishop's book, then, imagines first the mere tourist, then the invader, and finally, in the title poem, faces what is actually available to the traveller. "Questions of Travel" anticipates a new submissive understanding, taking what comes on its own terms, as she does with the magical powers of "The Riverman" or the mysterious quirks of the humble squatter-tenant, "Manuelzinho." The key to this new openness and affection is in the movement of the title poem. It proceeds through a cautious syntax of questions, with tentative answers in negative clauses. The glutted, excluded observer of the two opening poems ("There are too many waterfalls here") hallucinates mountains into capsized hulls, her own sense that travel might turn into shipwreck. Her first questions are asked with a guilty air: "Should we have stayed at home and thought of here? . . . Is it right to be watching strangers in a play . . . ?"

> What childishness is it that while there's a breath of life
> in our bodies, we are determined to rush
> to see the sun the other way around?
> The tiniest green hummingbird in the world?
> To stare at some inexplicable old stonework,
> inexplicable and impenetrable,
> at any view,
> instantly seen and always, always delightful?

You can hear Bishop's spirits rise to the bait of detail, the word "childishness" losing its air of self-accusation and turning before our eyes into something receptive, *childlike*, open to wonder. This is finally a less ambiguous approach than that of the traveller yearning to "look and look our infant sight away." "Questions of

Travel" does not expect, as "Over 2000 Illustrations" did, that vision will add up, restore our ancient home. The yearning remains ("Oh, must we dream our dreams / and have them, too?"). But the observer is drawn very cautiously by accumulating detail, and questions themselves begin to satisfy the imagining mind. The following passage, all questions, proceeds by the method Bishop admired in Darwin ("a self-forgetful, perfectly useless concentration"):

> But surely it would have been a pity
> not to have seen the trees along this road,
> really exaggerated in their beauty,
> not to have seen them gesturing
> like noble pantomimists, robed in pink.
> —Not to have had to stop for gas and heard
> the sad, two-noted, wooden tune
> of disparate wooden clogs
> carelessly clacking over
> a grease-stained filling-station floor.
> (In another country the clogs would all be tested.
> Each pair there would have identical pitch.)
> —A pity not to have heard
> the other, less primitive music of the fat brown bird
> who sings above the broken gasoline pump
> in a bamboo church of Jesuit baroque:
> three towers, five silver crosses.
> —Yes, a pity not to have pondered,
> blurr'dly and inconclusively,
> on what connection can exist for centuries
> between the crudest wooden footwear
> and, careful and finicky,
> the whittled fantasies of wooden cages.
> —Never to have studied history in
> the weak calligraphy of songbirds' cages.

Bishop has the structuralist's curiosity. She probably enjoys Levi-Strauss, who also studies "history in / the weak calligraphy of song-birds' cages" in the Brazil of *Tristes Tropiques*. Bishop rests in doubts, proceeds by a tantalizing chain of negative questions

(surely it would have been a pity . . . not to have seen . . . not
to have heard . . . not to have pondered . . . etc.). The closing
lines revisit the world of "Over 2000 Illustrations and a Complete
Concordance" but with more abandon, more trust to the apparent
randomness of travel and the state of homelessness:

> *"Is it lack of imagination that makes us come*
> *to imagined places, not just stay at home?*
> *Or could Pascal have been not entirely right*
> *about just sitting quietly in one's room?*
>
> *Continent, city, country, society:*
> *the choice is never wide and never free.*
> *And here, or there . . . No. Should we have stayed at home,*
> *wherever that may be?"*

I said earlier that details are also boundaries for Elizabeth
Bishop, that whatever radiant glimpses they afford, they are also
set at the vibrant limits of her descriptive powers. "In the Village"
and "Questions of Travel" show us what generates this precarious
state. "From this the poem springs," Wallace Stevens remarks.
"That we live in a place / That is not our own and, much more,
not ourselves / And hard it is in spite of blazoned days."[8] Bishop
writes under that star, aware of the smallness and dignity of human observation and contrivance. She sees with such a rooted,
piercing vision, so realistically, because she has never taken our
presence in the world as totally real.

4

"How had I come to be here?" Bishop asks in a recent poem, "In
the Waiting Room."[9] Even more than "In the Village," "In the
Waiting Room" invites us to understand Bishop's efforts in an
autobiographical light. Revisiting childhood experience, less open
to ecstasy than the earlier short story, "In the Waiting Room"
recalls the sense of personal loss so often implied behind Bishop's
observations. The poem is a melancholy visitation to a childhood
world Bishop has earlier ("In the Village") described more joy-

fully. This time she is accompanying her aunt to the dentist's office.

> while I waited I read
> the *National Geographic*
> (I could read) and carefully
> studied the photographs:
> the inside of a volcano,
> black, and full of ashes;
> then it was spilling over
> in rivulets of fire.
> Osa and Martin Johnson
> dressed in riding breeches,
> laced boots, and pith helmets.
> A dead man slung on a pole
> —"Long Pig," the caption said.
> Babies with pointed heads
> wound round and round with string;
> black, naked women with necks
> wound round and round with wire
> like the necks of light bulbs.
> Their breasts were horrifying.

The scream of "In the Village" is heard once again in a return to youthful memories of women in pain. But the scream, this time, is not banished.

> Suddenly, from inside,
> came an *oh!* of pain
> —Aunt Consuelo's voice—
> not very loud or long.
> I wasn't at all surprised;
> even then I knew she was
> a foolish, timid woman.
> I might have been embarrassed,
> but wasn't. What took me
> completely by surprise
> was that it was *me*:
> my voice, in my mouth.
> Without thinking at all
> I was my foolish aunt,
> I—we—were falling, falling,

> our eyes glued to the cover
> of the *National Geographic*,
> February, 1918.

The memory is astonishing, especially in the telling: the way in which "inside" allows us the little girl's own moment of confusion, as the cry seems to be her own. The child, entirely a spectator to others' pain "In the Village," finds unexpectedly that she is prey to it herself at the moment which sentences her to adulthood "In the Waiting Room."

Observation, the spectator's clear and lonely power, is a kind of life-jacket here. The poem is detailed and circumstantial: the child clings to details so as to keep from "sliding / beneath a big black wave, / another, and another."

> But I felt: you are an *I*
> you are an *Elizabeth*,
> you are one of *them*.
> Why should you be one, too?

The "I" that enters this poem, bearing her very name (the first time Bishop uses it in a poem) has the same staying power, no more, no less than the furniture of the waiting room, the arctics, the overcoats, the shadowy gray knees of the adults in the waiting room—all the sad imprisoning litany of human identity, like the numbers she takes pains to mention: three days until she is seven years old; the fifth of February, 1918. These read like incantations to "stop / the sensation of falling off / the round, turning world / into cold, blue-black space." The very plainness of the poem is what saves her; she is a realist *faute de mieux*, she observes because she has to.

"In the Waiting Room," like other poems Bishop has published since her *Complete Poems* appeared in 1969, rounds a remarkable corner in her career. My impression is that these pieces, collected in *Geography III* (1976), revisit her earlier poems as Bishop herself once visited tropical and polar zones, and that they refigure her work in wonderful ways. "Poem" looks to a small landscape by what must be the same great-uncle, an R.A., who painted the "Large Bad Picture" in her first book, *North & South*. "In the Waiting Room" revisits an awakening to adulthood as seen by a child, the world of "In the Village." "The Moose" recalls the pristine wonder of her Nova Scotia poems, and "Crusoe in England" looks back at a Southern hemisphere even more exotic than her tropical Brazil. In these and other poems, returning to earlier scenes, Bishop has asked more openly what energies fed, pressured, endangered and rewarded her chosen life of travel and clear vision.

Her "questions of travel" modulate now, almost imperceptibly, into questions of memory and loss. Attentive still to landscapes where one can feel the sweep and violence of encircling and eroding geological powers, poems such as "Crusoe in England" and "The Moose" pose their problems retrospectively. Crusoe lives an exile's life in civilized England, lord in imagination only of his "un-rediscovered, un-renamable island." In "The Moose" we are city-bound, on a bus trip away from Nova Scotia, and the long lean poem reads like a thread the narrator is laying through a maze—to find her way back?

"Crusoe in England" re-creates the pleasures and the pains of surviving in a universe of one. News that a new volcano has erupted trips Crusoe's memories of his own island. His way of thinking about it is that an island has been *born*:

> at first a breath of steam, ten miles away;
> and then a black fleck—basalt, probably—
> rose in the mate's binoculars
> and caught on the horizon like a fly.
> They named it. But my poor old island's still
> un-rediscovered, un-renamable.
> None of the books has ever got it right.

The shock of birth, the secret joy of naming, of knowing a place "un-renamable"—these emotions shadow the surface, as they do for the child of "In the Waiting Room." Crusoe's whole poem is pervaded by the play of curiosity. He asks questions, concentrates and then, as Bishop says elsewhere of Darwin, one sees him, "his eye fixed on facts and minute details, sinking or sliding giddily off into the unknown." The drifts of snail shells on Crusoe's island look from a distance like beds of irises. The next thing we know, they *are* iris beds:

>   The books
> I'd read were full of blanks;
> the poems—well, I tried
> reciting to my iris-beds,
> "They flash upon that inward eye,
> which is the bliss. . . ." The bliss of what?
> One of the first things that I did
> when I got back was look it up.

No point in finishing Wordsworth's quote: *imagination* would fill the blank better than *solitude* in this case, but neither is necessary in the presence of Crusoe's joy in the homemade and under the pressure of having to re-invent the world: "the parasol that took me such a time / remembering the way the ribs should go"; the baby goat dyed red with the island's one kind of berry "just to see / something a little different"; a flute, "Home-made, home-made! But aren't we all?" The poem is crowded with fresh experience: hissing turtles, small volcanoes. Crusoe has his longings— one fulfilled when Friday appears. He also has his nightmares. When he is on the island, he dreams about being trapped on infinite numbers of islands, each of which he must in painful detail explore. Back in England the nightmare is just the opposite: that such stimulation, imaginative curiosity and energy will peter out. His old knife ("it reeked of meaning, like a crucifix") seems to have lost its numinous power. The whole poem poses a question about imagination when it is no longer felt to be intimately related to survival. Bishop seems involved with the figure of Crusoe because of the questions *after* travel, a kind of "Dejection Ode" countered by the force and energy that memory has mustered for the rest of the poem. It acts out ways of overcoming and then re-experiencing loss.

Elizabeth Bishop has always written poetry to locate herself—most obviously when she is challenged by the exotic landscapes of North and South. She now performs her acts of location in new ways—sometimes showing the pains and joys of domestication, in poems like "Five Flights Up" and "12 O'Clock News" (the imaginative transformation of the writer's desk into a war-torn landscape). More important is the relocation in time, no longer seeing herself and her characters in long geological—Northern or tropical—perspectives, but in a landscape scaled down to memory and the inner bounds of a human life. What she finds are the pleasures and the fears of something like Crusoe's experience: the live memories of naming, the sudden lapse of formerly numinous figures. Early morning "Five Flights Up," listening to an exuberant dog in a yard next door, to a bird making questioning noises, she feels alive enough to imagine

> gray light streaking each bare branch,
> each single twig, along one side,
> making another tree, of glassy veins . . .

apart enough to conclude

> —Yesterday brought to today so lightly!
> (A yesterday I find almost impossible to lift.)

In another sense the past has its sustaining surprises. "Poem" is about the feelings awakened by a small painting passed down in her family, a landscape apparently by the great-uncle responsible for the "Large Bad Picture" which Bishop approached with diffidence and only submerged affection in *North & South*. In the new poem, the painter's work is welcomed as it brings alive, slowly, a scene from her childhood.

> I never knew him. We both knew this place,
> apparently, this literal small backwater,
> looked at it long enough to memorize it,
> our years apart. How strange. And it's still loved,

or its memory is (it must have changed a lot).
Our visions coincided—"visions" is
too serious a word—our looks, two looks:
art "copying from life" and life itself,
life and the memory of it so compressed
they've turned into each other. Which is which?
Life and the memory of it cramped,
dim, on a piece of Bristol board,
dim, but how live, how touching in detail
—the little that we get for free,
the little of our earthly trust. Not much.
About the size of our abidance
along with theirs: the munching cows,
the iris, crisp and shivering, the water
still standing from spring freshets,
the yet-to-be-dismantled elms, the geese.

I hear in these guarded, modest, still radiant lines a new note in
Bishop's work: a shared pleasure in imaginative intensity, almost
as if this remarkable writer were being surprised (you *hear* the surprise in her voice) at the power over loss and change which memory has given her writing. What else is it that we hear in "The
Moose," as the bus gets going through a lovingly remembered trip
from salt Nova Scotia and New Brunswick, world of her childhood, toward Boston where she now lives? The fog closes in, "its
cold, round crystals / form and slide and settle / in the white hens'
feathers." They seem to enter an enchanted forest, and she is
lulled to sleep by voices from the back of the bus, "talking the way
they talked / in the old featherbed, / peacefully, on and on." A
long chain of human speech reassures her: " 'Yes . . .' that peculiar / affirmative. 'Yes . . .' / A sharp indrawn breath, / half
groan, half acceptance." It is almost as if this discourse and its kinship to her own powers, the storyteller's powers handed down,
summon up the strange vision which stops the bus: a moose "tow-
ering, antlerless . . . grand, otherworldly"—primitive, but giving
everyone a "sweet / sensation of joy." It is "homely as a house /
(or, safe as houses)" like the very houses the quieting talk on the
bus recalls. The moose seems both to crystallize the silence, se-

curity and awe of the world being left behind and to guarantee a
nourishing and haunting place for it in memory.

In "The End of March" Bishop follows a looped cord along a de-
serted beach to a snarl of string the size of a man, rising and falling
on the waves, "sodden, giving up the ghost. . . . / A kite string?—
But no kite." It might be an emblem for these recent poems which
touch on lost or slender connections. Bishop seems more explicit
about that than she used to be. Where loss was previously the un-
named object against which the poems ventured forth, it is now
one of the named subjects. Her poems say out very naturally: "the
little that we get for free, / the little of our earthly trust. Not
much." Memory is her way of bringing to the surface and acknowledging as general the experience of losing which has always lain
behind her work and which the work attempts to counter. "One
Art" is the title Bishop gives to a late villanelle which encourages
these very connections.

> The art of losing isn't hard to master;
> so many things seem filled with the intent
> to be lost that their loss is no disaster.
>
> Lose something every day. Accept the fluster
> of lost door keys, the hour badly spent.
> The art of losing isn't hard to master.

The effort to control strong feeling is everywhere in this poem.
What falls away—love, homes, dreams—is hopelessly intertwined
with the repeating rhymes which challenge each other at every
turn: *master, disaster*.

> I lost my mother's watch. And look! my last, or
> next-to-last, of three loved houses went.
> The art of losing isn't hard to master.
>
> I lost two cities, lovely ones. And, vaster,
> some realms I owned, two rivers, a continent.
> I miss them, but it wasn't a disaster.

—Even losing you (the joking voice, a gesture
I love) I shan't have lied. It's evident
the art of losing's not too hard to master
though it may look like (*Write* it!) like disaster.

The last stubborn heartbreaking hesitation—"though it may look like (*Write* it!) like disaster"—carries the full burden, and finally confidence, of her work, the resolve which just barely masters emptiness and succeeds in filling out, tight-lipped, the form.

If Bishop's writing since *Complete Poems* still displays her tough idiosyncratic powers of observation, it also makes a place for those observations in very natural surroundings of the mind. The title *Geography III* (and its epigraph from "First Lessons in Geography") is at once a bow to her real-life relocation and a deep acknowledgment of the roots of these poems in childhood memory and loss. The time and the space these poems lay claim to are more peculiarly Elizabeth Bishop's own—less geological, less historical, less vastly natural; her poems are more openly inner landscapes than ever before.

II ROBERT LOWELL
The Uses of History

"Unerring Muse who makes the casual perfect": this is Robert Lowell's tribute to Elizabeth Bishop in a recent poem.[1] There is a lot to be learned from Lowell's admiration for a poet whose work is so entirely different from his own. In interviews, in public statements, he has often seemed full of yearning, ready to change his spots, to move toward the offhand, the unamplified statement. He remembers giving readings on the West Coast in March 1957: "I was still reading my old New Criticism religious symbolic poems, many published during the war," the poems which appeared in *Land of Unlikeness* and *Lord Weary's Castle*.

> I was in San Francisco, the era and setting of Allen Ginsberg, and all about very modest poets were waking up prophets. I became sorely aware of how few poems I had written, and that these few had been finished at the latest three or four years earlier. Their style seemed distant, symbol-ridden and willfully difficult. . . . I felt my old poems hid what they were really about, and many times offered a stiff, humorless and even impenetrable surface. I am no convert to the "beats." I know well too that the best poems are not necessarily poems that read aloud. . . . Still, my own poems seemed like prehistoric monsters dragged down into the bog and death by their ponderous armor. I was reciting what I no

41

longer felt. What influenced me more than San Francisco and reading aloud was that for some time I had been writing prose. I felt that the best style for poetry was none of the many poetic styles in English, but something like the prose of Chekhov or Flaubert.[2]

The book that emerged from these frustrations, *Life Studies* (1959), was explicitly autobiographical, growing out of Lowell's attempts to write a prose memoir (and indeed including a prose fragment in the first edition). Its final poem, "Skunk Hour," was dedicated to Elizabeth Bishop "because re-reading her suggested a way of breaking through the shell of my old manner."[3]

The poems in *Life Studies* do not sound like either Bishop or the Beats. If anything, their manner resembles that style of "scrupulous meanness" which Joyce chose for *Dubliners*—terse, unblinking, declarative and free of narrative comment. Bishop's work had reminded Lowell in "the qualities and abundance of its descriptive language . . . of the Russian novel."[4] There is not much of that descriptive generosity in *Life Studies*. But there is, in poems which touch on "the woe in marriage," mental illness and the frosty eccentricities of New England family life, the conviction that prose plainness must be his model—not because of Pound's dictum that all poetry should be at least as well written as prose, but rather from the compulsive belief that prose is "less cut off from life than poetry is."[5] Lowell speaks of the "ponderous armor" of his early poems, of the "shell" of his old manner, of his tendency to fall into a "mechanical, gristly, alliterative style that does not charm much, unless . . . I try to change my spots."[6]

Over the years the pressure toward and yearning for authenticity have been expressed with progressive intensity. Critics have come to see Lowell's enterprise almost entirely in those terms: "a long struggle to remove the mask, to make his speaker unequivocally himself."[7] Lowell's own self-descriptions encourage that view, but always wistfully, as if some yet greater immediacy were possible. He came to see *Life Studies* as catching "real memories in a fairly gentle style."[8] He had intended—and later felt it as a limitation—

that each poem in that book "might seem as open and single-surfaced as a photograph."[9] With *Notebook*, the poem he published and republished in two successive revisions over five years (1969-73), the object was more provisional: no "stills" as in *Life Studies*, but rather "the instant, sometimes changing to the lost. A flash of haiku to lighten the distant." "If I saw something one day, I wrote it that day, or the next, or the next. Things I felt or saw, or read were drift in the whirlpool, the squeeze of the sonnet and the loose ravel of blank verse."[10] A tone of gratitude and relief crosses Lowell's comments on the casual: "Accident threw up subjects, and the plot swallowed them—famished for human chances."[11]

Yet only three years after the revised *Notebook* appeared, in a publishing flourish no less-established poet could venture, most of the same poems, revised, with eighty or so new sonnets added, reappeared as *History*. "All the poems have been changed, some heavily. I have plotted. My old title, *Notebook*, was more accurate than I wished, i.e. the composition was jumbled. I hope this jumble or jungle is cleared—that I have cut the waste marble from the figure."[12] That Lowell should use the analogy of finished sculpture for *History*, that something as tentative as *Notebook* should grow into a larger, more resonant statement—everything implied by the title *History*—reveals one of Lowell's authentic temptations. He has been rewriting his poems from the very start, one book remaking poems from another. But *History* is the most ambitious of these ventures, the latest example of his desire to "make the casual perfect." We are in the presence of a continuing, baffling, often invigorating struggle in his work.

1

It is easy to portray Lowell's career as one of dramatic change: *Life Studies* marking a conversion to the urgent, the day-to-day, biography and autobiography. Lowell himself saw the book as a passage out of a period when "most good American poetry was a symbol hanging on a hatrack."[13] But *Life Studies* presents only one aspect of a career which has changed directions several times and whose appetites are complicated and contradictory. From the very start Lowell had been drawn to autobiographical poems of the sort that he wrote with more ease and success in *Life Studies* and *For the Union Dead*. The Winslows, his mother's family, enter his poetry as early as *Land of Unlikeness*, his Cummington Press book of 1944, and *Lord Weary's Castle* (1946), his first commercially published volume. There are lines specific and prosy enough to pass for later work: "Her Irish maids could never spoon out mush / Or orange-juice enough"; "Belle, the cat that used to rat / About my father's books, is dead." The story of how Lowell struck his father when he interfered in one of the young man's college love affairs was first told in *Lord Weary's Castle*, retold in the revision of *Notebook* and again in *History*, each time beginning in practically the same way: "There was rebellion, Father, and the door was slammed . . ."

Lowell's eagerness to incorporate autobiographical experience into his poems is not confined to an early, middle or late stage of his career. But it does have its seasons. He was to say after *Life Studies*: "I don't think that a personal history can go on forever, unless you're Walt Whitman and have a way with you. I feel I've done enough personal poetry. . . . I feel I haven't gotten down all my experience, or perhaps even the most important part, but I've said all I really have much inspiration to say, and more would just dilute. So that you need something more impersonal."[14]

We needn't take that statement as implying a simple boundary between public and private, though at least one critic, Patrick Cosgrave, is able to write confidently about *The Public Poetry of Robert Lowell*. Lowell "burns," according to Cosgrave, "to judge men and affairs against an immutable and objective standard."[15] *History* replaces *Notebook*, it is true. But Lowell doesn't move between public and private with the authority and ease of a Horace or a Pope. We are dealing with a troubled and prodigal poetic personality whose returns from private anxiety to draw a public breath are accompanied by overexposure and a certain conspicuous waste.

Historical judgment and public distance—the tone realized, for example, in "For the Union Dead"—are entangled with his own partly victimized awareness that he is a Lowell and a New Englander. He is, as Richard Poirier put it, "entrapped . . . among evidences of a past that promise but will not yield their secrets." It is in that sense that Poirier sees Lowell as "our truest historian." In his best poetry there is an unspoken and often intended plot: the ambition to write resonant public poetry is corroded again and again by private nightmare, by a failure to escape ghosts of the past. "The past, none of which he can reject or scarcely forget, exerts a control on his imagination, and his imagination, even while working to discover new and liberating possibilities in itself, can only be kept sane by reaching some understanding with the past."[16]

Lowell said that at the time he wrote *Life Studies* he didn't know whether it was a death-rope or a lifeline. His handling of autobiographical material since then suggests that he is still not ready—and perhaps need never be—to answer that question. The tone of *Life Studies*, flat and unadorned, was indeed a breakthrough. But his changes of manner since then, his likening *Life Studies* to still photographs, suggests that those poems did not solve the problem of authenticity, of a style adequate to the facts of his biography or his poetic ambitions. *Life Studies* poses questions about personal poetry and provides only one kind of answer, a solution to which Lowell did not remain committed. As with our reading of Bishop's poems, our problem with *Life Studies* is to identify the continuing drama behind the poetry's apparent lack of insistence, its apparently documentary surface. For Lowell, plain autobiography is an impulse, not an answer.

Perhaps the best way to frame a reading of *Life Studies* is to take examples from poems written before and since its publication. Among Lowell's earliest and latest works, though not his best, are attempts to deal with the moment when, as a young man, he struck his father. (This is an incident he does not touch in *Life Studies*, his first overtly autobiographical book.) There are three published versions. The first, "Rebellion," appears early in his career, in *Lord Weary's Castle*. Twenty years later, a significantly changed version appears in the "Charles River" sequence of *Notebook*, and again, only slightly revised, as "Father" in *History*.

All three versions are gnarled and go off in strange directions. But the first, "Rebellion," is *clearly* evasive. It veils most of its narrative in transferred action ("You damned my àrm" rather than "me").

> There was rebellion, father, when the mock
> French windows slammed and you hove backward, rammed
> Into your heirlooms, screens, a glass-cased clock,
> The highboy quaking to its toes. You damned
> My arm that cast your house upon your head
> And broke the chimney flintlock on your skull.

The *History* version keeps some of the evasiveness and transferred nervousness ("the highboy quaking to its toes"), but also opens to bluntness: "My Father . . ./I haven't lost heart to say *I knocked you down*." What is most noticeable in versions twenty years apart is the pressure in both cases to make the poem *signify*. Like many of the poems in *Lord Weary's Castle*, "Rebellion" sees human action on an apocalyptic scale. "Cast your house upon your head" bears an almost Biblical weight as well as the force of the young Lowell's anger against his New England Puritan and mercantile forebears. We know the mood from the poem which precedes "Rebellion" in *Lord Weary's Castle*, "Children of Light": "Our fathers wrung their bread from stocks and stones / And fenced their gardens with the Redman's bones. . . . They planted here the Serpent's seeds of light." Lowell stands aside, the avenging angel, in such bitter poems directed against tough old Yankee capitalism.

In "Rebellion" he tries to understand a moment of drama between father and son as part of that larger drama, an opportunity for the satirist's savage indignation against "the world that spreads

in pain." The young man dreams that the dead catch at his knees
and fall. And then

> Behemoth and Leviathan
> Devoured our mighty merchants. None could arm
> Or put to sea. O father, on my farm
> I added field to field
> And I have sealed
> An everlasting pact
> With Dives to contract
> The world that spreads in pain;
> But the world spread
> When the clubbed flintlock broke my father's brain.

The confusion of tenses at the end of the poem ("I have sealed
. . . But the world spread . . .") suggests awakened doubts, his
willingness to look again at the incident and see the whole poem
as a way of evading a primal rage. There is a shift, if a veiled one,
to take responsibility, to admit membership in the world he so
busily denounced: "But the world spread / When the clubbed
flintlock broke my father's brain."

Twenty years later the poem is revised to be part of a drama of
"witheredness"—to use a word Lowell applies to other later poems.
In *History* he uses several sonnets to take an expansive look at the
college love affair which provoked his assault on his father. The
context is now provided by poems in which he presents himself as
an aging father, haunted by the ghosts of his own parents, as in
"Returning":

> If, Mother and Daddy, you were to visit us
> still seeing you as beings, you'd not be welcome,
> as you sat here groping the scars of the house,
> spangling reminiscence with reproach

In "Father" the inescapable Oedipal tale fades into a tableau
from a hushed procession of fathers, as Lowell himself takes his
father's place.

> I have breathed the seclusion of the life-tight den,
> card laid on card until the pack is used,

> old Helios turning the houseplants to blondes,
> moondust blowing in the prowling eye—
> a parental sentence on each step misplaced. . . .
> You were further from Death than I am now—

"Devoted to surrealism," as Lowell claims to be in *Notebook*, successive revisions turn the original "glass-cased clock" into a less and less palpable furnishing. In *Notebook*, it is a "sun-disk clock," but in *History*, "your heirloom clock, the phases of the moon," as if to make the object itself transparent and through the figures of its decorated face to slip into the astrological certainty of the event. Images of exhaustion and process ("old Helios turning the houseplants to blondes") make parenthood seem to invite rebellion. With the end of the poem, Lowell abruptly shifts directions, and with no syntactical link, introduces a final mockery. The burned-out houseplants imagined as "blondes" lead to a sexual defiance from across the generation gap, delivered by

> that Student ageless in her green cloud of hash,
> her bed a mattress half a foot off floor . . .
> As far from us as her young breasts will stretch.

The momentary passing or "feel" of the incident becomes much less important to Lowell than the act of placing it in an elegiac context, a vein very congenial to him. The poem also allows him a half-ironic, half-yearning look at contemporary youth. My point is that entwined with the autobiographical impulse is a corresponding rhetorical effort to amplify events, to see them as part of the patterns of his past. In *History*, as in *Lord Weary's Castle*—but with far more humanity in the later version—Lowell refuses to trust a provisional account of this incident. We are not dealing, as some of his prefaces invite us to believe, with "the instant, sometimes changing to the lost."

I am concerned, then, with the varying autobiographical modes Lowell has devised throughout his career. Something in him resists the casual "I" of autobiography. Often, in his most interesting poems, counter-currents draw him away from any mere *present* he is trying to inhabit. In a poem like "Rebellion," and more successfully in "Children of Light," he tends to identify his personal anger with protests against hypocritical and prosperous New England Puritanism, as if satire could dispose of or resolve the quarrel with his personal past. The Catholicism he adopted at that time, as many critics have pointed out, was a peculiarly Calvinistic one, a platform from which he could denounce Boston and the mercantile life he made it stand for; all histories, personal and public, were instances of the Fall. Many of the poems of *Lord Weary's Castle* allow him to hold the past at a distance, as Boston hangs in the pans of judgment in "Where the Rainbow Ends." In the early poems he identifies himself with the finality of apocalyptic religious energy, as if this distancing were the only means he had to breathe and survive. This is a poetry of resonant judgments and memorable closing lines: "The blue kingfisher dives on you in fire"; "The Lord survives the rainbow of His will."

The force with which the younger Lowell saw the world and the past destroyed—poem after poem performed this gesture—was a reflex of their hold on him. No poetic mode was to be congenial unless he could, as Irvin Ehrenpreis puts it, "not only . . . treat himself as part of history but . . . treat history as part of himself."[17] How was he to incorporate what Ehrenpreis calls "the tone of fascinated disgust" (with society) into poems where, as at the close of "Rebellion," he begins to acknowledge his own nature, to feel himself alive and part of the world he denounces? How was he to find a voice which did not conceal his driven nature, his private grief and resentment, behind his social and religious stances? Was there an acceptable tone in which a poem might suggest historical judgments, but still reveal itself as the crazed glass of private vision? It was from this dilemma that Lowell describes himself emerging, with his "life studies" and especially with "Skunk Hour," which he called "the anchor poem in the sequence."

2

"Skunk Hour" was written in August and September 1957, after the California reading trip in which Lowell began to feel that his old poems "hid what they were really about." His account of writing the poem shows him at a crossroads. He wrote it backwards; the last two stanzas were, in point of composition, finished first, then the two preceding stanzas.[18] The admissions of mental breakdown ("My mind's not right") were on paper relatively early. But in its completed version, the poem opens with four satirical stanzas, introducing a decayed Maine village, which balance the four more "personal" stanzas Lowell had first composed.

He has performed a characteristic maneuver. The opening description, as Lowell put it, "gave my poem an earth to stand on, and space to breathe." It also allowed him, as the poem was written, to withdraw from psychological intensity into what seems at first glance to be wry social comment. "I found the bleak personal violence repellent. All was too close, though watching the lovers was not mine, but from an anecdote about Walt Whitman in his old age. I began to feel that real poetry came, not from fierce confessions, but from something almost meaningless but imagined."

In "Skunk Hour" Lowell was willing to forego the savage withdrawn irony of *Lord Weary's Castle* for a "more or less amiable picture." "Sterility howls through the scenery, but I try to give a tone of tolerance, humor, and randomness to the sad prospect. The composition drifts, its direction sinks out of sight into the casual, chancy arrangements of nature and decay."[19] Lowell seems aware that he *needs* this Maine landscape, but not as a platform of insulated moral judgment, the kind that separates the speaker from his world in angry poems like "Children of Light." Nor is it simply that a decaying Maine village offers a setting appropriately pathetic for the troubled "I" who enters undisguised in the fifth stanza. Looking at this landscape proves to be a challenge for the speaker. The satiric stanzas, at once smug and melancholy, are charged with his characteristic fears, later exposed and acknowledged. John Berryman was right in saying that "the poet is afraid of outliving himself,"[20] and that the opening stanzas glance apprehensively at figures who have gone away and at survivors who endure for nothing more than dotage and empty marriage.

Through the casual tones of the opening play a tune and rhythms which we later come to identify as the diseased speaker's own obsessive sounds: monosyllables with final and emphatic rhymes. "I myself am *hell*." "I hear / my *ill*-spirit sob in each blood *cell*." "The *hill*'s *skull*." Cars that lie together "*hull* to *hull*." Syllables like that have from the start been beating insistently through the poem.

> Nautilus Island's hermit
> heiress *still* lives through winter in her Spartan cottage;
> her sheep *still* graze above the sea.
> . . . .
> she buys up *all*
> the eyesores facing her shore,
> and lets them *fall*.
>
> The season's *ill*—
> we've lost our summer *mill*ionaire,
> who seemed to leap from an *L. L.* Bean
> catalogue. His nine-knot *yawl*
> was auctioned off to lobstermen.
> A red fox stain covers Blue *Hill*.

It is only at the fifth stanza that veils drop away and the dull inescapable toll is recognized for what it is. What we took for muted satire may or may not be objectively true; we come to see those opening stanzas tinged by the speaker's diseased vision as the poem goes on in the same throbbing sounds to reveal his disabilities.

> One dark night,
> my Tudor Ford climbed the hill's skull;
> I watched for love-cars. Lights turned down,
> they lay together, hull to hull,
> where the graveyard shelves on the town. . . .
> My mind's not right.
>
> A car radio bleats,
> "Love, O careless Love. . . ." I hear
> my ill-spirit sob in each blood cell,
> as if my hand were at its throat. . . .

I myself am hell;
nobody's here—

only skunks, that search
in the moonlight for a bite to eat.
They march on their soles up Main Street:
white stripes, moonstruck eyes' red fire
under the chalk-dry and spar spire
of the Trinitarian Church.

I stand on top
of our back steps and breahte the rich air—
a mother skunk with her column of kittens swills
        the garbage pail.
She jabs her wedge-head in a cup
of sour cream, drops her ostrich tail,
and will not scare.

Lowell's accomplishment in "Skunk Hour" is to have found a
tone which at once gestures toward larger meanings and yet allows
for the speaker's own crippling private nightmare. The opening
stanzas permit him his "fascinated disgust" with the world; the
later stanzas counter any impression of self-righteousness, of easy
world-weariness which the reader may be tempted to attribute to
him. How much he takes to himself the skunks, the crude defiant
survivors, is a difficult question. The casual half-rhymes and femi-
nine endings do give way to more resolute and emphatic stresses at
the close. The tone is partly one of amused relief and identification, though as John Berryman pointed out, it also encourages
absurd contrasts between the bold skunks and the human who admits his own terror: "I will. I *do* 'scare!' " It is, at any rate, clear
that in this poem Lowell moves toward a more exposed autobiographical style, one that does not mask his anger or disabilities behind apocalyptic rhetoric and social critique.

But, to see the nature of this exposure, it would help to look at a
poem typical of the barer "life studies." "Memories of West Street
and Lepke" shuttles back and forth between the comfortable Lowell living in Boston in the 1950s and his recall of the year he spent
in a New York jail as a conscientious objector.

> Only teaching on Tuesdays, book-worming
> in pajamas fresh from the washer each morning,
> I hog a whole house on Boston's
> "hardly passionate Marlborough Street,"
> where even the man
> scavenging filth in the back alley trash cans,
> has two children, a beach wagon, a helpmate,
> and is a "young Republican."
> I have a nine months' daughter,
> young enough to be my granddaughter.
> Like the sun she rises in her flame-flamingo infants' wear.
>
> These are the tranquillized *Fifties*,
> and I am forty. Ought I to regret my seedtime?
> I was a fire-breathing Catholic C.O.,
> and made my manic statement.

However plain the style, there is no mistaking the speaker for the apparently casual observer in Elizabeth Bishop's poems. Gabriel Pearson says of this and other *Life Studies* that "Lowell's treatment suggests not an exhibition but a cauterization of private material and emotion. Interest is not in what is revealed but in what is reserved."[21] No object in the poem seems to be allowed the independent interest often accorded by Bishop. Instead things bristle with an accusatory significance, all too relevant to the speaker, an "I" not at all relaxed or random in his self-presentation. So much of his experience is already second-hand, as in his self-conscious reference to what Henry James had long since identified as "hardly passionate Marlborough Street," an etiolated gesture toward an etiolated frame. Experiences seem preempted by rhetoric of the Eisenhower period ("agonizing reappraisal") or by advertising ("Like the sun she rises in her flame-flamingo infants' wear").

He talks about himself in implied ironic quotation marks. You imagine them around "fire-breathing" and "manic" in the lines "I was a fire-breathing Catholic C.O., / and made my manic statement." Line endings have a similar dry effect: "Given a year, / I walked on the roof of the West Street Jail . . ." The break forces a wry question; a momentary stepping back, *"given,"* indeed. This is the language of a man on trial, who hears words as if they belonged to someone else. "Fire-breathing" and "manic" are overheard characterizations, expressions he cannot adopt completely as his own. Prepared reactions of the "tranquillized Fifties" encrust his responses, make it hard to break through to feeling.

The distance between the speaker and his experience gives "Memories of West Street and Lepke" its special tension, the air that something is being withheld rather than yielded. So, for example, the mind seems to be making some flickering connection between the daughter's "flame-flamingo infants' wear" and the "seedtime" of the "fire-breathing Catholic C.O." It is a linguistic tease, not fully worked out. We are being asked to think about the "dragon" of a father, and the roseate daughter young enough to be his granddaughter, about a passage of vitality. Something is being suggested about failed ideology and the lapse into slogan-encapsulated domesticity of the 1950s and of middle age.

Gabriel Pearson tells us that in reading Lowell "we should notice how far . . . objects are re-apprehended and, as it were, redeemed for attention, by being locked and cemented into larger structures. They are never really innocent, autarchic objects like Williams's red wheelbarrow. They are there because they serve a significance or are at least apt for some design."[22] In "Memories of West Street and Lepke," Lowell seems to take very little primary pleasure in the objects named and remembered. The "pajamas fresh from the washer each morning" seem there not so much for themselves as to prepare our curiosity for a later detail, Czar Lepke, "piling towels on a rack." It is one of several parallels, teasing us into wondering what links the speaker in his laundered world to the boss of Murder Incorporated. Lowell remembers

> the T shirted back
> of *Murder Incorporated*'s Czar Lepke,
> there piling towels on a rack,
> or dawdling off to his little segregated cell full
> of things forbidden the common man:
> a portable radio, a dresser, two toy American

           flags tied together with a ribbon of Easter palm.
           Flabby, bald, lobotomized,
           he drifted in sheepish calm.

Both Lowell and Lepke belong to privileged worlds. The poet, hogging a whole house, remembers Lepke in "a segregated cell full / of things forbidden the common man." Outside, like the scavenger on Lowell's Marlborough Street, is the anarchic variety of the prison of which the younger Lowell was a part: "a Negro boy with curlicues / of marijuana in his hair"; Abramowitz, another pacifist. "Bioff and Brown, the Hollywood pimps," beat Abramowitz black and blue; it sounds like an energetic alliterative game to accompany Lowell from the tranquillized present to a busy, untidy past.

    Linked to the outlaw vividness, the young man glimpsed at its forbidden center Lepke. "Flabby, bald, lobotomized, / he drifted in a sheepish calm." A *doppelgänger* for the middle-aged speaker in his tranquillized forties, Lepke is an object of fastidious envy, if only for his pure preoccupation with death. Lepke, at least, is

           where no agonizing reappraisal
           jarred his concentration on the electric chair—
           hanging like an oasis in his air
           of lost connections. . . .

"Agonizing reappraisals" are the thieves of experience in the poet's world; Lepke's "lost connections" open to an oasis not visible on Marlborough Street.

    Or so the parallels and the patterns of the poem suggest. The arrangement of details and scenes invites us to make comparisons and contrasts upon which the poem itself deliberately makes no comment (not even to say, as Williams did, "The pure products of America go crazy"). Finally the poet's baffled failure to generalize becomes one of the subjects of the poem. The figures in the frieze have the air of being deliberately chosen and placed, deliberately recalled for the skilled analyst like key figures in a dream. Lost as the connections are between the criminal past and the respectable drugged present, the poem bristles with the challenge to recapture and unite them. Its selective organization teases us toward meaning, even if it is only in the form of a conundrum, a puzzle whose pieces we must match ourselves. Lowell pictures himself as becalmed; his poem, on the other hand, insists almost militantly on what Pearson calls the "vital chore of unremitting interrogation."

Over the years *Life Studies* has taught its readers how to interpret such poems as "Memories of West Street and Lepke," poems once characterized as random and flat. The short lines, the deliberately low-key vocabulary are ways of focusing our attention. Against such plainness a repeated gesture or word or color can take on unexpected resonance and can suggest obsessive connections between otherwise unlikely figures. "My Last Afternoon with Uncle Devereux Winslow" depends on a network of small details to reveal the fearful links between the five-and-a-half-year-old Lowell and his uncle, dying of Hodgkin's disease at twenty-nine. The child's wish to escape to imperishable death, his revulsion against his life full of relatives failing and dying—these feelings emerge slowly and by implication. It takes a reading as painstaking as Stephen Yenser's in *Circle to Circle* to interpret the seemingly meaningless details: the child picking away at a blue anchor on his white sailor blouse; the uncle also remembered in blue and white, about to "sail" for Europe on a last honeymoon before his death. The connections are latent, bristle with significance as in dreams, but as in dreams leave interpretation for afterward.

What happens within single poems happens in *Life Studies* as a whole. Poems in the opening sections throw up muted parallels and resonant images which prepare us for the Lowell autobiography in Part Four. Stephen Yenser speaks of Lowell's protagonists, some of them poets and friends, as "a line of alienated figures whose plights enforce and illuminate one another." He shows in an intricate argument the accumulating effect of figures like "A Mad

Negro Soldier Confined at Munich," Ford Madox Ford and Delmore Schwartz, whose fates rhyme with one another and allow Lowell eventually to associate "madness, war, and art."[23] How do *we* know to associate them with one another? Partly because of gathering small recurring details. (Yenser even links the "mustard spire" in "A Mad Negro Soldier" to the mustard gas in "Ford Madox Ford" and "For Delmore Schwartz.") Partly because of an almost musical construction. Yenser points out that, "In its tempo, its use of a persona whose sexual needs testify to estrangement from society, its mood of barely restrained violence, and its acerbic tone, and even in its position at the end of a section, 'Words for Hart Crane' is related to 'A Mad Negro Soldier Confined at Munich'; and at the same time, by virtue of all these features except the tempo, it is a forerunner of 'Skunk Hour.' "[24]

The critical reader, at some more or less conscious level, associates through memory these disparate experiences and images. It is important that the poet in his poems appears not to. Having recognized the glinting clues for what they are, he does not choose to let them come together directly in his poems. We may build readings, if only as a relief from the tension of recognizing details, situations and images which half rhyme with one another. Having done our critical detective work, having put the puzzle together, we always have to return to the poet's professed state of mind, the dispersal of clues as in a dream, the patient's report only just on the verge of interpretation. So, for example, much of the fear felt in connecting himself with Murder Incorporated's Czar Lepke must have been absorbed by the very discovery of an interrogatory structure which both linked them and kept them apart. It is Lowell's way of posing questions about his life without having, directly, to answer them.

3

Having tried to bring memories forward in *Life Studies*, Lowell often steps back to consider memory as a problem in his next book, *For the Union Dead* (1964). Writing autobiography brought

with it glimpses of chaos and nightmare: Lepke's inner eye
fixed on the electric chair; the crazed night cruiser of "Skunk
Hour"; the infantile bravado of the mental hospital of "Waking in
the Blue." It is no wonder that Lowell so often casts himself in a
distanced role, as a baffled spectator, sometimes as a voyeur. In
"Skunk Hour," behind the wheel of his Tudor Ford, he watches
for "love cars." In "For the Union Dead" he remembers how, as a
child, he stared through the aquarium's glass walls at "the dark
downward and vegetating kingdom / of the fish," his hand tingling to burst the bubbles from the "cowed, compliant fish." Later
in the same poem he is pressed against a barbed-wire fence to see
the "dinosaur steamshovels" devouring Boston Common for a new
parking garage. At the close of that poem, crouching before his
television set, he sees "the drained faces of Negro school-children
rise like balloons." The postures—and the poem itself—become a
screen between the poet and certain ungovernable experiences,
public and private. Present and past seem equally unavailable: the
"airy tanks" in the Boston Aquarium of his childhood, and the
faces of black children (on the TV news?) are equally "drained."
Or else, topsy-turvy, in another poem the poet himself drifts powerless and protected: "I swim like a minnow / behind my studio window." This is one image he finds for his baffled reaction to the
talk, "the chafe and jar / of nuclear war" in "Fall 1961."

It is clear even from a few examples that *For the Union Dead*
includes a network of observers and observed, one or the other behind glass. "The state / is a diver under a glass bell" ("Fall 1961").
The poems stand by themselves, but they also accumulate, in
waves of concentration and dispersal, a series of associations with
eyesight and vision. At the center of the book are accounts of
nightmares and dreams which have to do with the eyeglasses put
aside at night, with eye injuries and the memories they recall. In
"Myopia: a Night," without his glasses' aid and screen, Lowell
moves into a dream world of the present tense: "ramshackle,
streaky, weird / for the near-sighted." Its white "cell of learning"
gives no relief.

> . . . I hoped
> its blank, foregoing whiteness
> would burn away the blur,
> as my five senses clenched
> their teeth, thought stitched to thought,
> as through a needle's eye . . .

Instead he finds a dazzling Lucifer in his room, while his family's faces blur. "What has disturbed this household?"

In "The Flaw" he suffers from a mote in the eye (a hair on a contact lens?) and in "Eye and Tooth" an eye injury recalls an "old cut cornea." These too are ways of exploring and exposing his fragile position. In "Eye and Tooth":

> My whole eye was sunset red,
> the old cut cornea throbbed,
> I saw things darkly,
> as through an unwashed goldfish globe.

The lens through which he sees is a terrifying and necessary one. Seeing things "darkly," a parody prophet, he is both protected from and given carefully limited access to memories of an earlier lens:

> No ease for the boy at the keyhole,
> his telescope,
> when the women's white bodies flashed
> in the bathroom. Young, my eyes began to fail.

A physical affliction, by laconic juxtaposition, turns into a comment on childhood sexuality. The punishment is Biblical, too, an echo of what Moses prophesies for the dispersed children of Israel. Matching the inflamed eye of the poet is the eye of a "sharp-shinned hawk" remembered from a birdbook, another strict reminder of the Biblical laws of the fathers:

> clasping the abstract imperial sky.
> It says:
> *an eye for an eye,*
> *a tooth for a tooth.*

Memories of childhood are seldom innocent for Lowell. They almost always twin complicity (here, a boy's erotic games) and powerlessness (here, before the fantasy punishment). "No ease," the poem keeps saying. The adult present is described in past tenses. It is a shift to the present tense that brings back boyhood memories and threatens to overwhelm. "Eye and Tooth," like "Myopia," is a haunted poem, an extreme version of the baffled eye through which Lowell sees most experience in this volume. At some points flawed vision seems a punishment for opening ungovernable ranges of feeling. It can also be his protection. In "Eye and Tooth," "I saw things darkly, / as through an unwashed goldfish globe." What keeps "Eye and Tooth" together is that frail self-assertion, a tainted prophet who sets himself against the almost invincible Mosaic prophecies of his family which fill the rest of the poem. At the outset he is jaunty and self-deprecating, a neglected minnow in his unwashed bowl, or perhaps the ghost of a touring gypsy with a makeshift crystal ball. At the close he is wearied and wearying.

"Eye and Tooth" is a gloss on a pitiful and precarious situation. The book of which it is a part lifts often toward an optative mood, a wish to be transported back to immune pleasures of childhood. At least three times in *For the Union Dead* he invites someone or himself, directly, to "Remember." At other points, as in "The Lesson," the wish surfaces as exclamation and regret:

> No longer to lie reading *Tess of the d'Urbervilles*,
> while the high, mysterious squirrels
> rain small green branches on our sleep!

But the hedged wish is as far as he will go. He recalls "Those Before Us" warily, "in the corners of the eye," not straight on. Talking about those figures who lived in a familiar house is almost involuntary. They are "uniformly gray . . . They never were." Is this a way of keeping them securely dead? Or, as Stephen Yenser suggests, a sign of their vitality when they were alive: they never merely *were*.[25] In either case they represent spectral figures to

whom only momentary homage is offered. ("Bless the confidence /
of their sitting unguarded there in stocking feet.") Where he must
be "guarded," they are not. However much he wants to deny
them, they are present: "But in the silence, / some one lets out his
belt to breathe, some one / roams in negligee." There is a moment
of danger and violence in this uncontrollable past: "The muskrat
that took a slice of your thumb still huddles." It "furiously slashed
to matchwood" a packing crate, and, as a kind of surrogate for the
child, "learned to wait / for us playing dead" in a tin wastebasket,
before lashing out in terror. Powerlessness and complicity. In
grudging tribute to the family ghosts, "We follow their gunshy
shadows down the trail," part of their dying life. The end takes
place in that limbo where Lowell would like to cast most of his
memories: "Pardon them for existing. / We have stopped watching them. They have stopped watching." The mixture of regret and
relief is inescapable; the senses of "watch" multiply from *wariness*
to *care*.

4

Lowell recalls—with as much gusto as T. S. Eliot marshalled to say
it—a remark the older New England poet made to him at Har-
vard.[26]

> "Don't you loathe to be compared with your relatives?
> I do. I've just found two of mine reviewed by Poe.
> He wiped the floor with them˙ . . . and I was *delighted*."

Mischief is one way of handling the problem; insistence on an embalmed past is more often Lowell's. Memory, however much he
craves it, never has a nourishing or regenerative force for Lowell,
never the reviving power it has, classically, for Proust. There are no
madeleines in this world, only a past which has already been consumed. It is for this reason that many of the poems turn toward
elegy. "Always inside me is the child who died, / always inside me
is his will to die."

The lines are from "Night Sweat" and are followed by the
powerful, mysterious, idiosyncratic metaphor that Lowell develops

for the passage of memory into art: "one universe, one body . . . in this urn / the animal night sweats of the spirit burn." A resonant couplet, the emphatic close of the first two sonnets that make up this poem, the lines force together grim contradictory feelings. The "urn" contains the spent ashes of a dead childhood and, at the same time, the fevers of creation and nightmare. As the shell of the body, it is devoured by what it burns; as the urn of memory or verse, it preserves what is destroyed. If the lines are about transformation, the stress falls on what is consumed. What he captures is a fascinated repugnance. These are "the animal night sweats of the *spirit*," as if the Latin meanings ("spirit," "breath") behind the English *animal* were just barely still alive.

The images of "Night Sweat" are explored, and perhaps even generated, in the childhood recollections of "The Neo-Classical Urn," a poem printed earlier in the volume. It recalls, as Poirier says, "youthful callousness in which the poet recognizes his kinship both with 'turtles' and with the 'urn' in which, as a child, he threw them to suffer and die. The discovery of this metaphorical connection is itself the subject of the poem, as startling to the poet as it is to us."[27] The poetic stakes are high. He addresses the garden urn as if it were something out of Keats: "Oh neo-classical white urn, Oh nymph, / Oh lute!" The childhood he remembers at first sounds like an echo of Wordsworth, breathless, exhilarated, in a "season of joy":

> Rest!
> I could not rest. At full run on the curve,
> I left the cast stone statue of a nymph,
> her soaring armpits and her one bare breast,
> gray from the rain and graying in the shade,
> as on, on, in sun, the pathway now a dyke,
> I swerved between two water bogs,
> two seins of moss, and stopped to snatch
> the paint turtles on dead logs.

If this is Wordsworthian elation, it is rebuked as the turtles the boy collects are "dropped splashing in our garden urn." The

Wordsworthian catch falls into a Keatsian vessel "like money in the bank." The deflated allusions are there to suggest that romantic notions about childhood nourishing poetry are inadequate for this particular poet. His classical urn leads him to a new and terrifying version of the consumption of experience by art.

The poem moves along toward its remorseless discoveries with a series of separated but timely rhymes: childhood experience *hummed*; the pitiless boy who *strummed* the drowned beasts' elegy; the turtles which "popped up dead on the stale *scummed* / surface." The skull which recalls and which disowns its dead animal spirits is finally faced with acknowledging them as its own:

> nothings! Turtles! I rub my skull,
> that turtle shell,
> and breathe their dying smell,
> still watch their crippled last survivors pass,
> and hobble humpbacked through the grizzled grass.

A kinship is owned by the ambiguous subject of the last line (*turtles*, the first meaning, but also, the poet). Linked to "Night Sweat," the misery becomes clearer: "Always inside me is the child who died." The strenuous self-reflections in these poems are Lowell's deepest reports on an imagined monstrousness transformed, but not concealed or atoned, by art. This is, after all, the book in which he writes about his childhood identification with Caligula, th source of his nickname Cal.

So exposed, the sense of complicity and guilt rubs off on all relationships. In "Night Sweat" the tenderness with which he addresses his wife is touched by something else as well:

> your lightness alters everything,
> and tears the black web from the spider's sack,
> as your heart hops and flutters like a hare.
> Poor turtle, tortoise, if I cannot clear
> the surface of these troubled waters here,
> absolve me, help me, Dear Heart, as you bear
> this world's dead weight and cycle on your back.

Contact with his wife and child, with approaching day, is colored by shame and a plea for absolution. That much is clear, as is the reference back to the drowned turtles of "The Neo-Classical Urn." It remains a mystery whether "Poor turtle, tortoise" is a self-description (*tortoise:* the weighty antipode of the "hare" in the preceding line), in apposition to the drowning "I," or whether it is an endearment to his wife, an appeal touched by guilt. (In that case, the turtle which bears the universe on its back.) In either case, an openness to the self-consuming, even murderous animal spirits of the past has exhausted him.

These "night sweats" are partly the product of seeing ghosts. Memory of and by itself does not animate the present for him, as it does for writers like Wordsworth and Proust. On the contrary, it threatens to overwhelm him, to cut him off from the present and from his living wife and daughter. What are for other writers re-vitalizing links to childhood are not for Lowell one of the keys to an acknowledged and shared humanity. To redeem himself from monstrousness and isolation is to recognize the decaying mind and body as his links to humankind. The skull in "The Neo-Classical Urn" is the cerebral skull which at once consumes the animal spirits and is itself a death's head. In the tenderer, more human version of "Night Sweat" the urn of writing is also the body, self-consuming, self-embalming.

What I am getting at is that autobiography for Lowell is a prob-lematic form. He probes the reasons unflinchingly in these exposed dream poems at the center of *For the Union Dead*. Involuntary memory won't do. It is more congenial for him to write autobiog-raphy from the point of view of the elegist—experiencing himself and others almost entirely as members of Yeats's "dying genera-tions." "In truth," he says, "I seem to have felt mostly the joys of living; in remembering, in recording, thanks to the gift of the Muse, it is the pain."[28] Lowell gets a tainted joy from the notion that he is "reborn" in his writing. That discovery is repeated again and again in his work, most beautifully much later in *Notebook* and *History* in "Reading Myself":

No honeycomb is built without a bee
adding circle to circle, cell to cell,
the wax and honey of a mausoleum—
this round dome proves its maker is alive;
the corpse of the insect lives embalmed in honey,
prays that its perishable work live long
enough for the sweet-tooth bear to desecrate—
this open book . . . my open coffin.

5

The discoveries of *For the Union Dead* help us look forward and backward in understanding Lowell's way of writing about himself. In *Life Studies* he had left the evidence of the past on the edge of interpretation, for the reader to assemble. The details are there to be examined like dangerous radium particles, as by mechanical hands behind glass. Or, to change the metaphor and think of it from the poet's point of view, past and present are there like live wires, exposed but not to touch without insulation, as in "Memories of West Street and Lepke." The more exposed poems of *For the Union Dead* explore and explain why that insulation was necessary.

Lowell spoke of poems like "Myopia: a Night" and "Night Sweat" as writing "surrealism about my life." Five years later, in *Notebook*, he was to call surrealism his "method"—a way to accommodate tumultuous and threatening impulses, to drop his guard and visit the world where vision was as unclear as when he suffered his eye injury in "Eye and Tooth" or removed his glasses in "Myopia: a Night." The emerging poetry of *Notebook* went through several stages. Its publishing history re-enacts the struggles apparent in Lowell's poems all along. The *Notebook* of 1969 begins in a craving for immediacy: "Accident threw up subjects, and the plot swallowed them—famished for human chances." The *Notebook* fattened toward a revised edition in 1970; by 1973 it had become *History*.

Each of the editions has its own "Afterthought," and the crystallization of Lowell's sense of what he was doing is interesting to watch. There are modest reservations about the provisional and associative method from the start: "Surrealism can degenerate into meaningless clinical hallucinations, or worse into rhetorical machinery, yet it is a natural way to write our fictions."[29] A year later, in the revised *Notebook*, "surrealism" becomes "unrealism," and the cheering words about the "natural way" are replaced: "but the true unreal is about something, and eats from the abundance of reality." The appetite Lowell alludes to is the consuming appetite of plot, something which replaces and reorders the craving for less governable experience. In *History*: "All the poems have been changed, some heavily. I have plotted."

Lowell's "Afterthoughts" are an odd display of conflicting desires and views of poetry. Having risked disorder, he now decides that the composition of *Notebook* seems to him haphazard. On the other hand, critics, notably Stephen Yenser and Alan Williamson, have shown that *Notebook*, with all its scatter, had a plot—a plot which had to do with the stresses and the corrosive impulses that crack a marriage.[30] Many of those poems were cordoned off in two volumes which appeared simultaneously with *History*: *For Lizzie and Harriet* and *The Dolphin*, reflecting, in turn, a farewell to one marriage and a swimming free to another. What is interesting about *History* is not the distinction between plotted and plotless sequences so much as the plot which Lowell finally chose, the main view of his experience which Lowell was encouraged to take after mulling it over for almost five years. The image is from sculpture: "I have cut the waste marble from the figure." Stone jaws seem to close—as if after all the emotional untidiness of life in *Notebook*, a new protective and self-assertive posture were needed, placing the poet among the ruins of time.

The conversion of *Notebook* into *History* and its two attendant volumes was a bold, willful, utterly exposed gesture. Perhaps no poet since Whitman has made such continuous public revisions of his life. Yet Whitman accumulated everything he wrote into *Leaves of Grass*, as a way of making his book coterminous with his life; it would end only when he did. Lowell, on the contrary, performed a series of amputations and separations. Many of the events and sensations which prompted the Notebooks—his broken marriage, his taking a new wife—are themselves set apart in *For Lizzie and Harriet* and in some of the new poems of *The Dolphin*. *History* becomes much more his, the poet's, book, a codification of the elegist's position.

Still, it is hard to talk about *History* as if it were a book apart, since earlier versions of these poems are so much a matter of public record. With a career as ample as Lowell's the strenuous efforts at revising and re-ordering seem themselves to belong to the "complete works." Feelings experienced and developed in one context in *Notebook* are encountered in new and surprising guises in *History*. Sometimes, shorn of their original and more intimate connections, lines seem hollow. "Dispossession" began as a colloquy between husband and wife. It closed out a series called "Through the Night," prompted (this is conjecture) by an extramarital love affair in Cambridge, Massachusetts. The poem partly apologizes and partly explains the impulse to break the dream of continuing his marriage: "We are firemen smashing holes in our own house." Husband and wife yearn at the close

> . . . to swoop with the swallow's brute joy
> indestructible as mercy—the round green weed
> slipping free from the disappointment of the flower.

In *History* Lowell transfers this destructive yearning to a primarily political context, the decline of European aristocracies and the fall of the Romanoffs. Instead of "We are firemen," "The firemen smash holes in their own house." The last knotted lines of the sonnet are almost identical with the ones quoted above. But without the preparation of the situation in *Notebook*—the thwarted eroticism and broken marital dreams—the lines float free, *merely* powerful, but with little to resonate against.

I am not, by any stretch of the imagination, suggesting that *History* desexualizes Lowell's experience. But it does seem to provide a more rigorous and removed context for feelings which *Notebook* tells us were crystallized by marriage and love affairs. The dispersal of the seven sonnets entitled "Through the Night" in *Notebook* is a good illustration. Four of them appear under that same title in *For Lizzie and Harriet*. They take up the narrative center of the love affair with a younger woman. The others are separated in *History*: one, "Dispossession," follows a sonnet about the fate of the Romanoffs; one, "Vision," divorced from the specifically erotic context of "Through the Night," places its guilt among poems about the French Revolution. A third turns up in *History* as "Duc de Guise," the title it bears in all three versions. The poem is not much changed, except that it is cut loose from its old context of intimate pleasure and shame. In "Through the Night" it was a poem which looked back at the sexual encounter in Cambridge, prompted by the questioning guilt of the poem which preceded it: "Why was it ever worth my while?" The sonnet is full of anxiety about sexuality and growing older.

> The grip gets puffy, and water wears the stones—
> O to be always young among our friends,
> as one of the countless peers who graced the world
> with their murders and *joie de vivre*, made good
> in a hundred aimless amorous bondages. . . .

The fantasy of political power and sexual potency throws up the names of Achilles and the Duc de Guise. In *History* the poem follows a sonnet about Marlowe ("Tragedy is to die . . . / for that vacant parsonage, Posterity; / my plays are stamped in bronze, my life in tabloid"). It stands as a *memento mori* offered up to fantasies of erotic power:

> The irregular hero, Henri, Duc de Guise,
> Pope and Achilles of the Catholic League,
> whose canopy and cell I saw at Blois—
> just before he died, at the moment of orgasm,
> his round eyes, hysterical and wistful,
> a drugged bull breathing, a cool, well-pastured brain,
> the muscular slack of his stomach swelling
> as if he were pregnant . . . his small sword unable
> to encircle the circle of his killers.

There are two important revisions. The *small*, added to *sword* in *History*, intensifies a little the sexual humiliation. More important, the line was once "whose canopy and cell *we* saw at Blois." Now it is resolutely "I," nothing shared, nothing intimate about Lowell's tours of the psychic galleries of *History*. "Duc de Guise" is one of the most successful transplants from *Notebook*; it still bristles with its original anxieties and brutal feistiness. This remorseless crystallization of once intimate experience makes *History* the controlled nightmare it is. But then this is something Lowell announces from the start.

6

History opens as from a dream fraught with possibility. Lowell has written two new poems, and brought forward and revised several others to give the impression of someone wakening into the dawn of history. The book in fact moves forward chronologically: Biblical, Greek, Egyptian, Roman episodes and so on, to the present. But the volume is made to have a deeper logic. Someone is awakening: he has been counting sheep, watching the night out. Then adrift in "sweet sleep" he has heard "a voice / singing to me in French, '*O mon avril*.'" Then it is a pale Sunday morning in New York "and most cars dead." At this stage of the sequence (in "Bird?" and "Dawn") there is a sense of primitive promise and stir, or at least of alternatives to the mostly denatured world with which Lowell makes his peace later in the book.

"History has to live with what was here": the opening line of the volume. There are a number of ways to read it, including one that implies a defiant response: "History does, but I do not."

> History has to live with what was here,
> clutching and close to fumbling all we had—
> it is so dull and gruesome how we die,
> unlike writing, life never finishes.

The "finish" of writing is, albeit mockingly, *there*, a triumphant and brief flourish in the confusion of tenses which opens this

poem. This flash of the writer's alternative is, as always for Lowell, not comforting. He transforms momentary innocence or beauty
before our eyes into a death's head:

> As in our Bibles, white-faced, predatory,
> the beautiful, mist-drunken hunter's moon ascends—
> a child could give it a face: two holes, two holes,
> my eyes, my mouth, between them a skull's no-nose—
> O there's a terrifying innocence in my face
> drenched with the silver salvage of the mornfrost.

What is remarkable in these opening poems are the glimpses of
salvage, psychologically aligned with the drift from sleep into
dawn. Randall Jarrell said long before that Lowell "seems to be
condemned both to read history and to repeat it."[31] Once again on
the brink of that experience, he reaches out at the opening of *History* for exotic escape, unavailable but imagined—attempts to be
free of the *clutching* and *fumbling* which "history has to live with"
and which we have to live with in history. The "Bird?" of the third
sonnet is an extravagant prehistoric creature, a kind of feathered
apocalypse which killed the lizard tyrants "to a man." Identified as
"man's forerunner," it seems at once to destroy one historical age
and free us for another. Its primitive force is unavailable to him:

> I picked up stones, and hoped
> to snatch its crest, the crown, at last, and cross
> the perilous passage, sound in mind and body . . .
> often reaching the passage, seeing my thoughts
> stream on the water, as if I were cleaning fish.

In earlier versions, the dream was told in the present tense. Here it
occurs in the irrevocable past, and like the other poems which open
History, it envisions waste and dispersal—tantalizing, botched renewal.

Yet, as we move irrevocably into the daylight world after the
fall, there is a sense in which the opening dreamlike poems have established Lowell's independent presence. This is to be His-Story,[32]
the facts of the past to serve like a medieval mirror poem for private scares and edifications. He "performs" history, appropriates its

figures and events for self-confrontation, dream and nightmare. As
the historical pageant unfolds, he also takes his place in it, among
the perishable thousands this spectacle takes up and discards.

So, for example, in "Down the Nile." In *Notebook* this sonnet
was part of a sequence called "Long Summer," set in Castine,
Maine. Here it borrows a setting and a few lines, but drifts via a
"catalogue of ships" to an image from Egyptian paintings:

> those couples, one in love and marriage, swaying
> their children and their slaves the height of children,
> supple and gentle as giraffes or newts;
> the waist still willowy, the paint still fresh;
> decorum without conforming, no harness on
> the woman, and no armor on her husband,
> the red clay master with his feet of clay
> catwalking lightly to his conquests, leaving
> one model and dynasties of faithless copies—
> we aging downstream faster than a scepter can check.

The poem is all ease—the ease, for one thing, of Lowell's sonnets
which keep lines reasonably free of one another and allow him to
slip in and out of a scene with no syntactical link. He is, for a time,
a vicarious participant in the family life of the paintings, and then,
excluded and aging. The Egyptian husband is at first granted a
lovely immunity; "feet of clay" are quite naturally part of the picture for the "red clay master." "Catwalking" picks up the natural
suppleness of the giraffes and newts to which the children and
slaves are compared. At the outset it is all casual—no bondage, no
harness on the woman, no armor on the man. Then come the casu-
alties, as the attractive vocabulary of painted surfaces turns live to
remind us of the consequences of swagger and infidelity ("one
model and dynasties of faithless copies"). We return to the speaker's world. In the last line, veterans of modern marriage grow
older, powerless, baffled.

Lowell's sequence always returns us to history and its erosions.
The world of this book feels surprisingly like the world of *Lord
Weary's Castle*—more so than in any of Lowell's intermediate

works. But in this later panorama of decline and fall, the doomed
world of *History*, he is much more a participant, much less a witness. The perspectives are as stern and bleak as they were for the
Bostonian "Children of Light" in Lowell's first book. But now the
alternatives are different. The fallen world of *History* is ringed by
signs of a primitive vitality outlasting the willful tyrants, statesmen
and artists who emerge and vanish, as well as the poet who has
summoned up their ghosts. The bright ungovernable forces were
there at the start of the sequence, glimpsed but lost at the poet's
awakening—flashing outside human history, like the fierce creature
whose crest he cannot snatch in "Bird?." Creatures like these turn
up, mocking humans with an unavailable brute power of endur-
ance. In "Sounds in the Night," the insomniac poet can hear "the
grass-conservative cry of the cat in heat." "Cats will be here when
man is prehistory." Or, speaking to "Our Dead Poets," the poets
whose memories litter these pages:

> Sometimes for days I only hear your voices,
> the sun of summer will not adorn you again
> with her garment of new leaves and flowers . . .
> her *nostalgie de la boue* that shelters ape
> and protozoa from the rights of man.

Elegy modulates into bitterness and fear. In this context the
"rights of man" (and the "writings" as well, with which this sonnet begins) may sound downright murderous.

The alternative to senseless survival, to the "ape and protozoa,"
is the panorama of human arrangements which are the core of *History*, all of them to some degree seen as destructive and denatured:
politics, the family, marriage, art. In the harshest light all these activities have a common denominator, and Lowell, visiting his gallery of tyrants, heroes, lovers and artists, finds refractions of his
own thwarted and eroding powers. The old conqueror, Tambur-
laine, senile, gives a clue to their common ambitions:

> Timur . . . his pyramid half a million heads,
> one skull and then one brick and then one skull,

> live art that makes the Arc de Triomphe pale.
> Even a modernist must be new at times,
> not a parasite on his own tradition,
> its too healthy sleep that foreshadows death.
> A thing well done, even a pile of heads
> modestly planned to wilt before the builder,
> is art, if art is anything won from nature. . . .

The ambiguous "before"—wilting heads before the builder's eyes? or before the builder wilts?—cements a lurid identity between the tyrant's power and the consuming ambitions of a "modernist's" art. Lowell takes a sardonic and desperate view of what it costs a modernist—or at least one modernist—to win art from nature and build "his pyramid."

One of the first things the sleeping poet sees as he wakes into history is Orpheus bringing tumult into Eden. The construction of "In Genesis" makes it seem as if it is Orpheus who enacts original sin, rather than the serpent, Adam and Eve, who "knew their nakedness, / a discovery to be repeated many times . . . / in joy-less stupor?" Unlike them

> Orpheus in Genesis
> hacked words from brute sound, and taught men English,
> plucked all the flowers, deflowered all the girls
> with the overemphasis of a father.
> He used too many words, his sons killed him,
> dancing with grateful gaiety round the cookout.

"In Genesis" was originally titled "Out of the Picture," one of the last poems in *Notebook*. Now it stands almost as a headpiece to *History*, a way of entering from the natural and primitive dawn into a poet's awareness of history. It places him, as most of the book does, among the consuming and consumed, downplaying at every turn any myth of the nourishing power of art.

What Lowell has finally put on display is a universe as severe as that of his early religious poems, but stripped of their theology and carved out of his own literary experience. As Stephen Yenser points out, *History* "contains, and is to some extent informed by, poems from all of Lowell's previous volumes."[33] Lowell's identifications with literary and historical figures have been gathering for years— sometimes directly through his historical poems and literary imitations. At other times, writing autobiography has allowed him to discover historical parallels to his own experience. The crystallization of *History* out of *Notebook* is only the latest stage in a steady dialogue, an attempt to place unruly and threatening experience into an understandable pattern. Now the parallels are marched out in chronological order, fraught with his own reflected meanings, a framework in which he can judge himself in turn as husband, lover, son and poet.

It would be interesting to trace in detail the refractions, the enactments and re-enactments, of those roles as they are unfolded in *History*. Here I can only suggest some of the accumulated effects. Marriage, for example, is tugged free of the autobiographical frame of *Notebook* and is in some senses explored with more immediacy through dramatic characters in whom the poet can concentrate one or another aspect. "Solomon's Wisdom" began in *Notebook* as "The Book of Wisdom," a poem more noticeably about Lowell, tied to the facts of his life ("Can I go on loving anyone at fifty," it began). In *History*, slightly revised, it concentrates more pointedly on desire and aging. Seen through Solomon's eyes, what was once only a weary modern complaint takes on the conflated air of erotic fantasy and nightmare: " 'Can I go on keeping a hundred wives at fifty?' " At the close:

> "King Solomon croaking, *This too is vanity*;
> *her lips are a scarlet thread, her breasts are towers—*
> hymns of the terrible organ in decay."

This poem takes its place—marriage under the aspect of aging and multiplying desires—in the gallery alongside poems like "Milton in Separation," where marriage is seen under the aspect of a writer's vocation: "His wife was no loss to the cool and Christian Homer." A poem like "Marriage" (in *Notebook*, "The Bond"), where Lowell speaks in his own voice and not through a dramatic character, still takes on an air of finality in *History*. Apart from the eddy and flow of daily incident, its context now is more completely provided by "Milton in Separation," which preceded it and in which writing feeds on the distance between the epic poet and his wife. In "Marriage":

> Too long we've hungered for its ancient fruit,
> marriage with its naked artifice;
> two practised animals, and close to widow
> and widower, greedily bending forward
> for a last handgrasp of vermillion leaves,
> clinging like bloodclots to the smitten branch—
> fibrous growths . . . green, sweet, golden, black.

It should perhaps be no surprise that the poems of *For Lizzie and Harriet* should have been set apart, published with *The Dolphin*, almost as appendices. These small books are the illustrations, the extended glosses, the particular instances of the tenderness and betrayals which are remorselessly judged, and placed, once and for all out of the sphere of accident and turmoil in *History*.

As with marriage, so too with the family vicissitudes Lowell explored in *Life Studies* and later—and especially his role as son. Those psychological trials are notably distanced and re-enacted in the anger, violence and bravado of a remarkable series of dramatic monologues on Clytemnestra and the murder of Agamemnon. The poems are all the more effective placed close to the beginning of the volume, to the sense of awakening from a dream into the nightmare of history. In that twilight area of the book, it is as if we were encountering family energies in their rawest form. Later those energies are met in muted contexts, remarkably in a series which reviews and re-orders the incident in which Lowell knocked his father down for interfering in a college love affair. I have described earlier Lowell's obsessive returns to poems dealing with that experience. In *History* the episode finds what is probably its final context and its final form, a placement and refiguration which make it securely part of what Philip Levine calls "the entranced procession of the dead."

"You were further from Death than I am now," Lowell says as he takes the place of the remembered father. "I have breathed the seclusion of the life-tight den." "Father" has come the way of many of the poems adapted from *Notebook*. There it was almost incidental, recalled as he talked about a Cambridge love affair of the 1960s in a sequence called "Charles River." The sonnets dealing with that later sexual encounter are cut from *History* and dispersed. "Father" is brought forward, and now, with a title, takes its place in a long sequence dealing with his parents, leading to two reunions with his father, one of which used to be called "My Death."

It would be pointless to multiply examples of the way Lowell has made *History* the elegiac autobiography he seems to have been searching for so long. His tribute to Elizabeth Bishop, "unerring Muse who makes the casual perfect," does as much to mark his distance from her as it tells about the loosening influence she and others have had upon him. Lowell's moves toward the provisional in poetry have often been guarded and, as far as a feeling of renewal is concerned, unavailing, as in *Life Studies*. His moves toward the private world have been accompanied by nightmare, as reflected in *For the Union Dead*. Bishop's relaxation leads her, like her favorite Darwin, to a vision of geological and ecological order, albeit one which ultimately excludes her. Lowell's relaxation leads to a more monstrous Darwinian world outside human history, either indifferent to us or a projection of our worst nightmares. History, as Lowell sees it, is made up of the monuments men build to escape their inhuman selves, the mocking order men make from human fear and will. Being part of it is the only way Lowell finds to authenticate his life—an ultimate arrogance, but one in which he is as remorseless to himself as he is to others.

III   JAMES MERRILL
Transparent Things

Toy ukelele, terrorstruck
Chord, the strings so taut, so few—
Tingling I hugged my pillow. *Pluck*
Some deep nerve went. I knew

That life was fiction in disguise.
                              "Days of 1935"

A child's dream, gaily recalled in James Merrill's "Days of 1935," is one of the best introductions to his work. Not that the motto "Life was fiction in disguise" can be extracted harmlessly, like an infant tooth, from this poem, a modern ballad, both mysterious and disingenuous in tone. The ballad's neat appetite for experience almost shrugs away what others raise their voices to assert. Still the tantalizing proposition remains. Many of Merrill's poems, weightier than "Days of 1935," return to fictions believed in childhood, later fleshed out by life: "Lost in Translation," "Matinees," "Chimes for Yahya," "The Broken Home." It is one of the things which makes his writing about himself so different from Robert Lowell's. A continuing access to childhood memories and insights nourishes Merrill's verse; with Lowell, the memories are most often terrifying and unavailing.

In Merrill's "Days of 1935" a child dreams of being kidnapped by Floyd and Jean, a gunman and his gum-chewing moll, rough parodies of Bonnie and Clyde. Their peculiar combination of fairy-tale and silver-screen glamor makes the child hope that he will never be ransomed. More than that, the openly exotic and erotic ménage transforms his bed on the floor into a magic carpet.

> The rag rug, a rainbow threadbare,
> Was soft as down. For good or bad
> I felt her watching from her chair
> As no one ever had.

Someone watching him, someone to watch: he spends a whole day telling fairy tales to the astonished Jean, himself astonished. "I stared at her—*she* was the child!" With Floyd and Jean the whole forbidden parental world is exposed to eye and ear:

> One night I woke to hear the room
> Filled with crickets—no, bedsprings.
> My eyes dilated in the gloom,
> My ears made out things.
>
> Jean: The kid, he's still awake . . .
> Floyd: Time he learned . . . Oh baby . . . God . . .
> Their prone tango, for my sake,
> Grew intense and proud.
>
> And one night—pure "Belshazzar's Feast"
> When the slave-girl is found out—
> She cowered, face a white blaze ("Beast!")
> From his royal clout.

Fantasies fulfilled, a star-struck child learns what romance violence stands for, and makes the inevitable connections with the tensions behind the etched, hieratic world of his parents:

> Photographs too. My mother gloved,
> Hatted, bepearled, chin deep in fur.
> Dad glowering—was it true he loved
> Others beside her?
>
> Eerie, speaking likenesses.
> One positively heard her mild
> Voice temper some slow burn of his,
> "Not before the child."

The daytime world to which he eventually returns is two-dimensional, by comparison with his red-blooded imaginings. His parents' guests, in a series of brilliant puns, are rendered as cartoon cut-outs, devitalized:

> Tel & Tel executives,
> Heads of Cellophane or Tin,
> With their animated wives
> Are due on the 6:10.

The energy to see them this way comes from the boy's own discovered vitality, his storytelling powers. The child sees sparks fly across the gap between truth and fiction: his invented kidnappers expose his parents to him in new ways, and allow him, later on in the poem, a glimpse into the indulgences and inhibitions put upon his own erotic life.

Part of the pleasure here lies in reclaiming banner headlines of the 1930s and film fantasies of the 1960s for the psychic life from which they spring. In the ballad form, the secrets of childhood, dreams of conquest and revenge, unfold with the ease and inevitability of nursery rhymes. And through fiction his parents become available to him in ways never possible in life.

That Merrill is writing a kind of autobiography in verse—however different from Lowell's or from so-called "confessional" poetry—becomes clearer with each of his books. "The Book of Ephraim" in *Divine Comedies* is only the most explicit and extended of these efforts. Yet it is also clear that Merrill is not engaged in capturing the raw momentary feel of experience in the present tense (what Lowell claimed to be doing in his first *Notebook*). The poems perform that continuing revision of a poet's life through his work to which many autobiographical writers are committed. But, as "Days of 1935" suggests, Merrill's poems come close to day-to-day living by discovering the fantasies behind our civilized arrangements, our secret links to fiction.

1

Like Lowell, Merrill has absorbed into verse many of the resources of daily conversation and prose. Still, there is a special strangeness and sometimes strain to Merrill's colloquial style, a taut alertness to the meanings which lurk in apparently casual words and phrases. We may find this in all good poets, but Merrill raises it to a habit of vigilance, a quickened control and poise, sometimes bravado, which he clearly trusts as a source of power. When Merrill uses an idiom, he turns it over curiously, as if prospecting for ore. So, for example, the dead metaphor "on the rocks" springs unexpectedly to life in this section from "The Broken Home," a poem which anticipates the family strains of "Days of 1935."

> When my parents were younger this was a popular act:
> A veiled woman would leap from an electric, wine-dark car
> To the steps of no matter what—the Senate or the Ritz Bar—
> And bodily, at newsreel speed, attack
>
> No matter whom—Al Smith or José Maria Sert
> Or Clemenceau—veins standing out on her throat
> As she yelled *War mongerer! Pig! Give us the vote!*,
> And would have to be hauled away in her hobble skirt.
>
> What had the man done? Oh, made history.
> Her business (he had implied) was giving birth,
> Tending the house, mending the socks.
>
> Always the same old story—
> Father Time and Mother Earth,
> A marriage on the rocks.

All conversational ease and, at the end, outrageous humor, Merrill's wit allows us momentary relaxation and then plants its sting. This newsreel is one of the central panels of an often saddened and erotically charged work. The cartoon suffragettes and their male oppressors prove more than quaint in the context of a long poem whose speaker is exorcizing the ghosts of a broken home. Behind the gossip columnist's phrase ("on the rocks": shipwreck dismissed as if it were a cocktail) lies a buried colloquial truth about the tensions eternally repeated in a worldly marriage, Father Time and Mother Earth, re-enacted erosions and cross-purposes. Beneath amused glimpses of 1920s bravado, the verse penetrates to parents' energies (both envied and resented) that shape and cripple a child's.

> How intensely people used to feel!
> Like metal poured at the close of a proletarian novel,
> Refined and glowing from the crucible,
> I see those two hearts, I'm afraid,
> Still. Cool here in the graveyard of good and evil,
> They are even so to be honored and obeyed.

Merrill's absorption of prose rhythms and colloquial idioms has something of the structuralist's curiosity behind it, an interest in casual observations which both veil and betray buried feelings. In "Up and Down" Mother and son are alone in a bank vault to inspect her safe-deposit box: "She opens it. Security. Will. Deed." The puns are telling. The wit is there to reveal patterns that vein a life: a precarious and double use of ordinary speech much like the quality Merrill admires in the poetry of the contemporary Italian Montale, some of whose work he has translated. He speaks of Montale's

> emotional refinement, gloomy and strongly curbed. It's surprisingly permeable by quite ordinary objects—ladles, hens, pianos, half-read letters. To me he's *the* twentieth-century nature poet. Any word can lead you from the kitchen-garden into really inhuman depths. . . . The two natures were always one, but it takes an extraordinary poet to make us feel that, feel it in our spines.[1]

With this in mind we can begin to understand Merrill's peculiarities as an autobiographical writer: his sense of the dual accountability of poetry to the "two natures," to daily life and to the "really inhuman depths."

Merrill's best poetry from *Water Street* (1962) on is autobiographical in more than accidental and local detail. Figures and places recur. The mother of "Up and Down" is the mother recalled in "The Broken Home" and "Lost in Translation." Kyria Kleo, the Greek maid, returns in "After the Fire" after her intro-

duction in "Days of 1964." "Days of 1935" playfully refers us to
"Days of 1971." But the place of narrative detail in Merrill's work
is like the timely progress of a love affair behind a sonnet sequence.
It is not so much what happens that counts, or the exterior order
of events, the frame-by-frame record. It is the cumulative power of
specific entrances and exits, the psychic resonance which key figures, places and objects come to possess. The figures who appear
and re-appear in Merrill's poems have more substance than the
legendary heroines who were muses to the sonneteers, but they also
have the same mesmerizing force, as he considers and reconsiders
their shaping impact on his life. To reread Merrill's books since
Water Street is to discover him preparing a stage whose objects
and cast of characters become increasingly luminous. They become
charged with symbolic meaning and release symbolic reverbera-
tions from otherwise ordinary narrative event.

Take this playful insight into the psychopathology of everyday
life, "The Midnight Snack," one of the "Five Old Favorites" in
Water Street:

> When I was little and he was riled
> It never entered my father's head
> Not to flare up, roar and turn red.
> Mother kept cool and smiled.
>
> Now every night I tiptoe straight
> Through my darkened kitchen for
> The refrigerator door—
> It opens, the inviolate!
>
> Illumined as in dreams I take
> A glass of milk, a piece of cake,
> Then stealthily retire,
>
> Mindful of how the gas-stove's black—
> Browed pilot eye's blue fire
> Burns into my turned back.

The casual tone, the deft rhyming, the detachment of the sonnet,
the triviality of the ostensible subject, all play against the real

feeling—one small exploration of stolen pleasure in the presence of inhibition. The trick is in the handling of objects, allowing an apparently easy concentration to awaken the presences he feels in such a scene. It is all over before we have time to sort out our sense that wires have been crossed: the association of cold with nourishment and mother; of warmth with anger and father. Merrill hasn't had to resort to that psychic underlining. "You hardly ever need to *state* your feelings. The point is to feel and keep the eyes open. Then what you feel is expressed, is mimed back at you by the scene. A room, a landscape. I'd go a step further. We don't *know* what we feel until we see it distanced by this kind of translation."[2]

Much of Merrill's interest in narrative and everyday experience has been aimed at discovering the charges with which certain objects have become invested for him. He seems in his developed poetry to be asking the Freudian or the Proustian question: what animates certain scenes—and not others—for us? Over the years Merrill's poems have used the objects and stages of daily life, the arrangements of civilized behavior, almost as if he expected to waken sleeping presences and take by surprise the myths he lives by. It is not for nothing that he admires Joyce and Cocteau: "Joyce teaches us to immerse the mythical elements in a well-known setting; Cocteau teaches us to immerse them in a contemporary spoken idiom."[3]

2

But it took Merrill time to discover the vocabulary and gestures which would coax out the inner meaning of his experience. The conviction that "life was fiction in disguise" charges his poetry from the very start. Yet *First Poems* (1951) and *The Country of a Thousand Years of Peace* (1959) stand apart. These are books in which Merrill is continually interrogating presences as if they were on the edge of eternity. *First Poems* is a lonely and tantalizing collection, whose characteristic speaker is a solitary, often a child, attempting to decipher or translate elusive natural emblems: a shell, periwinkles, a peacock. These poems address themselves, frustrated and transfixed, to scenes on the brink of transformation: the secretive "Periwinkles" whose insides are "all pearled / With nourishment sucked out from the pulsing world"; or, in "Transfigured Bird," a child toying with the "eggshell of appearance" which, blown empty, "is void of all but pearl-on-pearl / Reflections." Many of these poems take up the matter of going beyond appearances so earnestly as to make *First Poems* seem "last" poems as well. Still, behind the conversational ease and realism of Merrill's subsequent books is the feeling which animates the very first poem of this one, "The Black Swan": the child's yearning to see the world symbolically. It haunts, informs and strengthens everything he writes.

By the time of *The Country of a Thousand Years of Peace*—eight years had passed since *First Poems*—the solitary speaker had become a world traveller. Yet that worldly grounding only licenses and confirms his questions about the solidity of appearances. He is less interested in what the traveller sees and more in his distanced way of seeing things. Japan, India, Holland, Greece: the journey only confirms him in the feelings of exile and strangeness expressed in *First Poems*. The "country of a thousand years of peace" is Switzerland, where the young Dutch poet, Hans Lodeizen (1924-50), a friend almost Merrill's own age, died of leukemia. Lodeizen is the "necessary angel" of the book, as he is to be again a tutelary figure in the later "Book of Ephraim." The title poem and the final dedicatory verse of *Country* are addressed to him, and the true country of both the title and the book is "that starry land / Under the world, which no one sees / Without a death."

It is in *Water Street* that Merrill commits himself to his brand of autobiography and, with a title as specific as his previous had been general, turns his poetry toward a "local habitation and a name." The occasion of the book is moving to a new house. The closing poem of the book, "A Tenancy," settles him in Stonington, Connecticut, on the village street of the title, in the house which is to be a central presence in his work. The move confirms him in poetic directions he had already begun to follow: "If I am host at

last / It is of little more than my own past. / May others be at
home in it." *Water Street* opens with "An Urban Convalescence,"
a poem which dismantles a life in New York City where life is
continually dismantling itself. Merrill's move is inseparable from
the desire to stabilize memory, to draw poetry closer to autobiography, to explore his life, writing out of "the dull need to make
some kind of house / Out of the life lived, out of the love spent."

The domesticating impulse closes both "An Urban Convalescence" and "A Tenancy" and effectively frames the book. Imagined as dwelling places, the poems are at once new creations and
dedications to what is durable, salvageable from the past. They
emerge as signs of Merrill's deep and nourishing debt to Proust,
whose work he had admired since his undergraduate days and had
now found a way to absorb. There is a poem "For Proust" in
Water Street, but Proust's mark is everywhere in the poems about
the continuing presence of childhood memories.

In "Scenes of Childhood" a motion-picture projector, more explicitly realistic and Freudian than Proust's magic lantern, has the
same power to resuscitate a personal past. A son and his mother
go through the obsessive psychic replays which home movies permit and symbolize. They watch the mother in younger days, her
sisters with plucked brows, and then the son as a child of four. A
man's shadow "mounts" the mother's dress. The child breaks into
tears, becomes a little fury. "The man's shadow afflicts us both."
As they try to slow down the film it jams.

> Our headstrong old projector
> Glares at the scene which promptly
> Catches fire.
>
> Puzzled, we watch ourselves
> Turn red and black, gone up
> In a puff of smoke . . .
>
>   . . . Alone
> I gradually fade and cool.

Old movies silently fan old Oedipal flames and become indistinguishable from inner experience. There are no distanced emblems to be interpreted here, as there were in Merrill's earlier poems. The poet is at once overheated projector and the childhood he projects, part of the flow of images ("Father already fading— / Who focused your life long / Through little frames"). The anguish revived by the experience in "Scenes of Childhood" is not clearly resolved or dispelled as it is to be in later poems, but the manner of the poem is important. In his first two books Merrill had imagined the riddling objects and landscapes of nature and his travels as teasing him, just on the edge of releasing hidden meanings. They were stable, static, as if seen on a photographic negative or on an etcher's plate ("images of images . . . insights of the mind in sleep"). In *Water Street* the optical image is extended to motion-picture films and refined to accommodate mysteries interior and fleeting, stored in memory, only to be glimpsed in motion and discovered by activating the charged details of our own lives.

It is here that the author of *Remembrance of Things Past* is most clearly Merrill's master. Proust writes in *Time Recaptured* of the power of memory—involuntary memory—to awaken the riddling presences of the world.

> But let a sound, a scent already heard and breathed in the past be heard and breathed anew, simultaneously in the present and in the past, real without being actual, ideal without being abstract, then instantly the permanent and characteristic essence hidden in things is freed and our true being which has for long seemed dead but was not so in other ways awakes and revives, thanks to this celestial nourishment.[4]

Merrill was to say of his own habits of composition: "When I don't like a poem I'm writing, I don't look any more into the human components. I look more to the *setting*—a room, the objects in it. I think that objects are very subtle reflectors."[5] The best poems in *Water Street* are about the conditions under which the past becomes truly available and nourishing. What landscapes, what objects will, in Wallace Stevens's word, "suffice"?

"An Urban Convalescence" begins with an illness and ends in a resolute separation from New York, a gesture fulfilled by the "Tenancy" on *Water Street* which closes the book. Out for a walk in Manhattan after a week in bed, the poet falls into dazed self-questioning. Demolitions are going on in his block: he wonders "what building stood here. Was there a building at all? . . . Wait. Yes. . . . Or am I confusing it . . . ?" Soon the subject becomes memory itself. A garland remembered from the lintel of a demolished New York doorway leads back to a cheap engraving of garlands in which he had wrapped a bouquet presented to a now-forgotten Paris romance:

> Wait. No. Her name, her features
> Lie toppled underneath that year's fashions.
> The words she must have spoken, setting her face
> To fluttering like a veil, I cannot hear now,
> Let alone understand.

Forgotten faces are like forgotten fashions ("fluttering like a veil") and like the demolitions which began the poem ("toppled underneath that year's fashions"). By this point objects and setting have become so naturally entangled with inner experience that every statement widens to include memory or forgetfulness. The garland whose roots he spoke of earlier and whose memory re-awakened the bouquet of flowers and the Paris romance ends with a truncated echo in the pock-marked walls exposed by the demolitions. "Wires and pipes, snapped off at the roots, quiver. / Well, that is what life does." His surroundings epitomize his own sense of failed connections and disintegrated personality.

> So that I am already on the stair,
> As it were, of where I lived,
> When the whole structure shudders at my tread
> And soundlessly collapses.

"An Urban Convalescence" is designed to act out a false start and implicitly to suggest a search for more revealing and durable images. What he appears to be learning to do is to disentangle his own needs and style from the clichés of the world of fashionable destruction—a clarification of feeling signalled in the crisp rhymed quatrains from this point to the end of the poem. It ends with the implied resolve to find new and resonant settings in his memory.

> back into my imagination
> The city glides, like cities seen from the air,
> Mere smoke and sparkle to the passenger
> Having in mind another destination
>
> Which now is not that honey-slow descent
> Of the Champs-Elysées, her hand in his,
> But the dull need to make some kind of house
> Out of the life lived, out of the love spent.

Much of the poem's feeling is gathered in the now charged associations of *house*: the perpetual dangers of exposure and change, of fashion and modishness; the sifting of memory for patterns which will truly suffice. "An Urban Convalescence" is just such a sifting of memory. Entangling inner and outer experience, it leads us to see the poem itself as potentially a "house," a set of arrangements for survival or, to use Merrill's later phrase, for "braving the elements." Poems were to make sense of the past as a shelter or a dwelling place for the present.

In future poems, other houses were to become charged conductors of meaning—shelters explored, destroyed, mended, invoked; reflectors for glimpsing the larger patterns of his life. Among them: "The Broken Home"; his childhood house, "18 West 11th St.," destroyed by Weathermen making bombs; the love-scarred Athens house of "After the Fire"; the slumbering house in "Under Libra"; Psyche's house in "From the Cupola"; the Stonington house with its stardeck in "The Book of Ephraim."

But Merrill had probably begun to prepare this stage as early as the mysterious piece which closes *First Poems*. Called simply "The House," it goes without grammatical break from title to opening lines

Whose west walls take the sunset like a blow
Will have turned the other cheek by morning, though
The long night falls between, as wise men know:

Wherein the wind, that daily we forgot,
Comes mixed with rain and, while we seek it not,
Appears against our faces to have sought

The contours of a listener in night air,
His profile bent as from pale windows where
Soberly once he learned what houses were.

A house "turns the other cheek." Wind takes—or makes—the shape of "a listener in night air," who seems like a solitary bending from pale windows. With no syntactical breaks—and a confusing fluency—the poem dissolves ordinary boundaries between interior and exterior landscapes, the idea of "house" rendered completely metaphorical, like an astrological house. Nor are *inside* and *outside* the "house" distinct locations. We experience the "house" almost as a transparency, a shelter improvised against a larger exposure: "Night is a cold house, a narrow doorway."

I have entered, nevertheless,

And seen the wet-faced sleepers the winds take
To heart; have felt their dreadful profits break
Beyond my seeing: at a glance they wake.

What one feels in that dreamlike situation is, as Merrill was later to identify it, "something like the sleeping furies at the beginning of 'The Eumenides'—only as embodiments of the suffering they bring. An early example of elements braved?"[6] The particular houses Merrill writes about in later poems—however real, solidly located and furnished—are also imagined as vulnerable houses of the spirit. They are never mere settings. In the details he uses to conjure them up, there are always reminders of the particular kinds of exposure and emergency against which these domestic arrangements have been contrived. It is not simply that they displace confining dwellings of the past—the broken parental home,

the narrow apartments of false starts. The very act of choosing
what spaces, attributes, solid elements of the house to invoke *becomes* the action of the poem. A transparency of setting characterizes Merrill's writing, bleaching out distracting, merely accidental
details and fixing most of his houses as improvised houses of survival and desire.

But in *Water Street*, the most powerful poems are those stressing
the exposures against which Merrill's dwellings were to be devised.
"An Urban Convalescence" is the best known of these poems, but
"Childlessness" is probably the most important. "Childlessness"
draws together narrative impulse and symbolic framework so violently that it seems not to fuse but confound them. Here, in a
phantasmagoric landscape, houses "look blindly on"; the one glim-
mering light is not the poet's own.

> The weather of this winter night, my dream-wife
> Ranting and raining, wakes me. Her cloak blown back
> To show the lining's dull lead foil
> Sweeps along asphalt.

Richard Saez has spoken of Merrill's "wrested comparisons." No
paraphrase could do justice to the uncomfortable marriage of poet
and Nature which permeates this poem. Whether he is thinking of
Nature as fostering the children he does not have or as infusing
the visions of art, he remains battered between dream and nightmare. What is played out is a stormy version of the cool drama
enacted much later with the mother in "Up and Down." In that
later poem the mother gives her son an emerald his dead father
had given her when their child was born.

> I do not tell her, it would sound theatrical,
> *Indeed this green room's mine, my very life.*
> *We are each other's; there will be no wife;*
> *The little feet that patter here are metrical.*
>
> But onto her worn knuckle slip the ring.
> Wear it for me, I silently entreat,

> Until—until the time comes. Our eyes meet.
> The world beneath the world is brightening.

This later poem includes self-mockery and self-possession; above all, it is secure about an unspoken understanding between mother and son. "Childlessness," written ten years earlier, is more distraught, less resolved. At its close, the dawn is "A sky stained red, a world / Clad only in rags, threadbare."

> A world. The cloak thrown down for it to wear
> In token of past servitude
> Has fallen onto the shoulders of my parents
> Whom it is eating to the bone.

The poem, because of its fierce freedom to move from level to level, to be both household drama and natural perspective, can include matters of individual guilt and responsibility, but can also transcend them. It conflates a number of views of Nature's gifts. The cloak which at the end consumes his parents like the shirt of Nessus is, at the beginning, part of the description of the winter night and belongs to his "dream-wife," the wintry weather. At times experience is measured on a human scale: Nature is a fantasy mate, a figure at different points accusing (nothing is planted in his childless "garden"), absolving, nourishing and tempting. But the conceit, once seized, opens a world of more mysterious operations among presences which dwarf and outlive us. The poem moves through a section of rapid and dizzying transformations:

> I lie and think about the rain,
> How it has been drawn up from the impure ocean,
> From gardens lightly, deliberately tainted;
> How it falls back, time after time,
> Through poisons visible at sunset
> When the enchantress, masked as friend, unfurls
> Entire bolts of voluminous pistachio,
> Saffron, and rose.
> These, as I fall back to sleep,
> And other slow colors clothe me, glide
> To rest, then burst along my limbs like buds,
> Like bombs from the navigator's vantage,

> Waking me, lulling me. Later I am shown
> The erased metropolis reassembled
> On sampans, freighted each
> With toddlers, holy dolls, dead ancestors.
> One tiny monkey puzzles over fruit.

The transformations are hard to keep track of; the refusal to allow experience to settle is part of the poem's point. Nature's cloak and the consuming cloak at the end of the poem are closely related to the bolts of material in this passage. The exotic colors of sunset, distilled from the storm, first *clothe* the poet, then *burst* along his limbs like *buds*. The image is meant to counter an earlier one: that nothing is planted in his garden (no natural blooms, like children). Then the *buds* become *bombs*, and the reward for being on target is a curious miniaturization of the world. A bombed metropolis is reassembled on sampans, a decimating version of the powers of art. The dream ends, as a *stained* dawn replaces the exotic dyes of sunset. Unlike those tropical shades, dawn's colors do not clothe him. For hours he cannot *stand* (both "bear" and "rise") to *own* the threadbare world—or to face its alternative: the cloak, a token for his parents who performed the expected service to nature. Their reward is also what devours them.

This is one of Merrill's most exposed poems, anticipated in the closing lines of "An Urban Convalescence." It offers rapid and conflicting perspectives against which to view the particulars of human feeling. Childlessness, guilt and suffering are set within the framework of nature's ample violence, its mysterious ecology, its occasionally exalting cyclical promise and power. Merrill has discovered a stage which will accommodate surrealistic effects released by a familiar domestic situation. The effect is like an opening out of space, a large corrective for moments of individual exposure. Merrill forces leaps from the "kitchen garden" to "really inhuman depths," the poetic gift he admired in Montale. But he also seems uncomfortable with these accesses of power. In "Childlessness" the technique is abrupt and insistent, a prey sometimes to strained self-justification or exaggerated guilt. It finds no way to

separate the bareness and power of his own life from the punishment of his parents. And so the poem never really settles; at the
close it comes to rest rather than resolution. Shuttling, adjusting
perspectives constantly as we must to read this poem, we hear a
mixture of self-accusation, self-delight and defiance. In the final
lines the parents, consumed to the bone, are introduced with a
baffling combination of bitterness, contrition and fierce confrontation with the way of the world. What happens violently in "Childlessness" happens with more meditative certainty later in his
career.

3

In "Childlessness" and other poems from *Water Street* Merrill
moves toward more overtly autobiographical work. *Nights and
Days* (1966), the next book, is the classic Merrill volume—jaunty,
penetrating and secure. It contains some of his best poems, though
later works were to be richer, more searching, high-flying, even
shocking and relaxed. But several of the poems in *Nights and Days*
are paradigms of how he was going to use autobiographical details
in his poetry. Or to reverse it, in Merrill's own words, how the poet
was to become a man "choosing the words he lives by."

"Time" is a poem about that process. It begins with a dazzling
ambitious sentence, full of the bravado of a talented young poet
finding outrageous metaphors for Time:

> Ever that Everest
> Among concepts, as prize for fruitful
> Grapplings with which
> The solved cross-word puzzle has now and then
> Eclipsed Blake's "Sun-Flower"
> (Not that one wanted a letter changed in either)
> And jazz believed at seventeen
> So parodied the slopes
> That one mistook the mountain for a cloud . . .

The verse paragraph is itself a kind of pastime with its outrageous
etymology for Everest and its breathy syntax. The seductively lib-
erated fantasy transforms games of Patience into

Fifty-two chromosomes permitting
Trillions of 'lives'—some few
Trimphant, the majority
Blocked, doomed, yet satisfying, too,
In that with each, before starting over,
You could inquire beneath
The snowfield, the vine-monogram, the pattern
Of winged cyclists, to where the flaw lay
Crocus-clean, a trail inching between
Sheer heights and drops, and reach what might have been.

He starts out as a plucky adventurer, sure about the larger human curiosity which card games (and poems!—Blake's "Sun-Flower") stand for and the kinds of fear they overcome. In the lost game of Patience, you can still peek at the blocked cards and get a God's-eye view of the pitfalls.

Against that bravado play the voices of everyday life, what is possible—voices of the son who postpones his life and the father who nags at him:

He grasped your pulse in his big gray-haired hand,
Crevasses opening, numb azure. *Wait*
He breathed and glittered: *You'll regret*
You want to   Read my will first   Don't
Your old father   All he has   Be yours

With the entrance of the father, the imagined adventures of the poem's opening turn into something more dangerous: "Crevasses opening." An emerging vision—still cards, still mountain-climbing—is more mysterious, tempered by the long littleness of life. The father fades into a figure like Father Time and also becomes a distant peak, his features "ice-crowned,—tanned—by what?— / Landmark." The son, a fitful dreamer "smoothing the foothills of the sheet," has a new image of his journey:

You take up your worn pack.

Above their gay crusaders' dress
The monarchs' mouths are pinched and bleak.

> Staggering forth in ranks of less and less
> Related cards, condemned to the mystique
>
> Of a redeeming One,
> An Ace to lead them home, sword, stave, and axe,
> Power, Riches, Love, a place to lay them down
> In dreamless heaps, the reds, the blacks,
>
> Old Adams and gray Eves
> Escort you still.

Without dropping his original vocabulary of pastimes, Merrill is exposed to a widening vision of what pastimes really are, how they are linked to ambition and faith eroded by time. The technique here as elsewhere is one of bold transformations: the "worn pack" of eternal card games merges with the mountain climber's burdensome pack. Tested against the experience of the beleaguered, procrastinating son, the images of the opening reveal unexpected depth and dimension. It is as if a curtain rises for the mesmerized speaker. Or as if the blinding defensive component of wit had fallen away. The surface royalty of the cards drops off "in dreamless heaps, the reds, the blacks, / Old Adams and gray Eves." Once triumphant they are now "condemned to the mystique / Of a redeeming One."

What is particularly remarkable is the way the poem is pitched toward discovery and makes us go through the process. As in "Childlessness" (though with less anger) he sees his surroundings, his daily experience, in an ever deepening perspective, though this time one *shared* by demanding father and reluctant son. In the son's drifting vision, the father actually *becomes* the landscape, the "ice-crowned . . . / Landmark," at the end of his journey. Meditated long enough, a dramatic situation, a scene, a landscape, even an object become transparent, like the pack of cards melting into the tired traveller's "worn pack." Merrill is committed to such unfolding images and to the puns which reveal them. "Time" acts as a rebuke to the gamesman at the opening of the poem, dwarfs his defenses, offers him a glimpse of the deep corrective wisdom of language.

I have said that *Nights and Days* is the classic Merrill volume. From this point on he seems entirely secure about the relation of his poems to autobiography and memory, to social surface and colloquial language. The security is reflected in pieces which begin or end with explicit references to writing, several in this volume: "The Thousand and Second Night," "The Broken Home" and "From the Cupola." (In later volumes, poems like "Yánnina," "Under Libra" and "Lost in Translation.") The poet will be seen at his desk, looking back at an encounter or a crisis, or in the heat of events will glance forward to the time when he is alone and unpressured. Merrill is as committed as other writers included here to capturing the immediate feel of experience, but often insistent that writing is part of that experience. Or, to put it his way, "What you feel is expressed, is mimed back at you by the scene. A room, a landscape. I'd go a step further. We don't *know* what we feel until we see it distanced by this kind of translation." The "translation" of which he speaks marks him off from the authors of *Leaflets* and *Notebook*. One thinks of Adrienne Rich's burning impatience with the way writing fixes experience ("A language is the map of our failures"), her preference for the provisional, the ever more authentic, and the present tense. In *Notebook* Lowell wanted "the instant, sometimes changing to the lost." For Merrill there is the experience and the settling in of the experience; "the blackbird whistling / or just after," as Stevens puts it.

Merrill is suspicious of the straightforward first-person present indicative active: "this addictive, self-centered immediacy, harder to break oneself of than cigarettes."

> That kind of talk . . . calls to mind a speaker suspicious of words, in great boots, chain-smoking, Getting It Down On Paper. He'll never notice "Whose woods these are I think I know" gliding backwards through the room, or "Longtemps

je me suis couché de bonne heure" plumping a cushion in-
vitingly at her side. . . . Think how often poems in the
first-person present begin with a veil drawn, a sublimation of
the active voice or the indicative mood, as if some ritual
effacement of the ego were needed before one could go on.
"I wonder, by my troth, what thou and I . . ."; "Let us go
then you and I. . . ." The poet isn't always the hero of a
movie who *does* this, *does* that. He is a man choosing the
words he lives by.[7]

These words are from an interview which accompanied the first
publication of "Yánnina," a poem which ends with the poet at his
desk as an intense experience slowly takes form in his mind. The
quote suggests the conviction with which Merrill accepts the notions of poetic closure and the composed self—notions which many
writers of autobiographical verse would suspect as artificial, false
to the provisional nature of things. In many of Merrill's poems,
the closing is also the point at which the poem opens out, as
"Time" unfolds a new perspective in which to view the poet's
actions and anxieties.

Merrill prefers poems in the first-person present which begin
"with a veil drawn" ("a sublimation of the active voice or the indicative mood . . . a ritual effacement of the ego"). That attitude helps explain the presence of a short poem as prologue to
each of his later books. In particular, "Nightgown," "Log" and
"Kimono" are small ritual prefaces,[8] overheard, propitiatory,
modest, veiled overtures of poet to Muse. "Nightgown," the short
invocation to *Nights and Days*, is typical of their modest tone and
function:

> A cold so keen,
> My speech unfurls tonight
> As from the chattering teeth
> Of a sewing-machine.
>
> Whom words appear to warm,
> Dear heart, wear mine. Come forth
> Wound in their flimsy white
> And give it form.

Prompted by exposure, writing begins as a form of slender protection. However commonplace the material, however awkward the gestures (the chattering teeth), words not only *seem* to warm but, in a second sense of *appear*, their express purpose is to warm the heart. The homely effort lures out an informing spirit: a poem's emergence signalled in the rapid shift in the last two lines from the disparate plural of words to the singular white form, *their* to *it*. Everything happens as a trust in process; the poem, homespun nightgown, eventually becomes the dreamer's garb.

The warming lure of words is a recurring form of invocation for Merrill. He introduces it, for example, into the beginning of "The Broken Home," summoning a *tongue* of fire in his cool sunless room ("a brimming / Saucer of wax, marbly and dim— / I have lit what's left of my life"). In "From the Cupola" the fiery tongues are those of the senses, "a certain smouldering five / Deep in the ash of something I survive." In that case, as in "The Broken Home," the fuel for the poem is the self, and the speaker a survivor who is there not only to tell his story, record a shock, but also to show how recollection probes an experience to release its larger meaning.

Richard Saez, in a brilliant description of the effect of some of Merrill's long poems, notes that:

> Each poem begins after a physical or emotional crisis has enervated the poet, effecting something like Proust's intensified sensibility after an asthmatic attack. A delicate but incisive sensuous perception leads from the present to related scenes in the past. . . . Movement is more in the rhythm of ritual dance—measured, repeated steps with darkly significant variations—than narrative action . . . eroticism is closer to the core than to the surface. When the focus has narrowed sufficiently to burn through the poet's self-absorption, remaining under the thin gauze of ashes is the poem: a cooling artifice which coalesces and refigures the past.[9]

Saez has conflated two of Merrill's own metaphors for the effect of poems: from "Log," the gauze of ash which remains "after the fire"; and, from "Days of 1971," the description of a miniature glass horse from Venice. The latter is a token from a now fading love affair, unwrapped at the end of the trip that concludes things between the lovers:

> Two ounces of white heat
> Twirled and tweezered into shape,
>
> Ecco! another fanciful
> Little horse, still blushing, set to cool.

The feelings of a no-longer-driven lover are inseparable from, are indeed discovered in, an image which has to do with ending a love poem. The love token suggests a miniature Pegasus. The mixture of unfulfilled love and unfulfilled anger spills over into mixed feelings about the poem: a sense of rueful accomplishment, of embarrassed pleasure ("still blushing"), of diminution, life miniaturized and "set to cool."

In other poems—say, "The Broken Home"—the cooling less irritably refigures the past. I wouldn't say of such works, as Saez does, that "fire—in any of its many forms—is more the protagonist than the poet who observes and meditates." But certainly the repeated motifs of aroused flames and cooling attune us to an intensity of involvement seemingly at odds with the almost deadpan wit and surface detachment of many of the poems. As readers we have to be aware of the verbal "layers" of a Merrill poem: his way of shadowing plots beneath the narrative surface and suggesting the complex involvement of the ego in any given experience. While the civilized storyteller takes us into his confidence, adjustments of time, temperature, light and background call attention to his own emotional activity and psychic experience of the poem.

"The Broken Home" shows that double movement at its clearest. The home is the one he grew up in, but also one we are given to feel *he* breaks within the poem. We must watch two actions at the same time. In one, the poem seems like a series of slides of the past, each a sonnet long, presenting the characters of his Oedipal tale and encounters between them. In the other action, the present tense of the poem, we watch the poet lighting his scenes. Behind these surfaces, changes of timing, brightness and scale render the scenes as transparencies. Or, to put it another way, the changes in his writing, the heightened temperature of involvement, coax out an inner experience. It is as if a poem required a kind of scrim among its resources, before or behind which action may be seen in new configurations as new beams of light are introduced.

To be specific: "The Broken Home" opens in the present with a set of contrasts. The poet has seen the family upstairs posed in their window in static tableau and as if with an overlaid fire ("gleaming like fruit / With evening's mild gold leaf"). Against this, the poet's own solitary room on the floor below is sunless, cooler, but potentially alive with an inner turbulence. Countering the waxen still life above, his room is "a brimming / Saucer of wax, marbly and dim," capable of generating a series of images from the past of his own very different sense of family. "I have lit what's left of my life." The problem of "Childlessness" is here acted out in a more controlled manner. "Tell me, tongue of fire, / That you and I are as real / At least as the people upstairs." On the surface the approach is oblique, a series of sonnets. Each detaches itself from the one before, seems to force a new start, appears to approach but skirt danger: a satiric portrait of his father; the projection of his mother's feelings into a vignette of angry suffragettes; next, a central panel of the poem, an openly erotic scene when the child enters his mother's darkened bedroom, the scene ending in a terse cartoon ("The dog slumped to the floor. She reached for me. I fled").

But we are drawn as into a labyrinth, away from detached and generalizing pasts ("My father, who had flown in World War I, / Might have continued to invest his life / In cloud banks well above Wall Street and wife"). By the fifth sonnet the poem shades from an immediate past into an eternal present: "Tonight they have stepped out onto the gravel. / The party is over."

A lead soldier guards my windowsill:
Khaki rifle, uniform, and face.
Something in me grows heavy, silvery, pliable.

How intensely people used to feel!
Like metal poured at the close of a proletarian novel,
Refined and glowing from the crucible,
I see those two hearts, I'm afraid,
Still. Cool here in the graveyard of good and evil,
They are even so to be honored and obeyed.

The images are radiant and confusing. They tap emotions which
have as much to do with getting past his own witty defenses (that
toy lead soldier is, among other things, a guard) as with the knotted explosive family triangle. In the poem's power to woo and
summon taboos, there is a release full of contradictions of identity.
It is the two hearts of the parents which are with prime authenticity "Like metal poured at the close of a proletarian novel." Or
is the son, earlier like a melting lead soldier, "heavy, silvery, pliable," also passing through the crucible and, by virtue of the experience, able to "see those two hearts . . . still"? The enjambed syntax is part of enjambed feelings and allows both interpretations.
What has been kept separate before is here interlocked, all and
forever present "in the graveyard of good and evil."

The passage, like the most intense moments in poetry, won't
hold still before the eye. Depending on your phrasing, "How intensely people used to feel" links forward and puts the parents at
an envied anachronistic distance ("Like metal poured at the close
of a proletarian novel"). Or the phrase links backward, identifying
the son with his parents in a shared deep focus. Seeing double
works here because the feelings which are almost fused have, in
the earlier part of the poem, been held so long in provocative tension. To follow one set of flickering clues: the poet's room at the
opening is sunless and cool. Despite his invoking a "tongue of
fire," the following sonnets are oddly distanced. The father is remembered through "smoked glass" ("The soul eclipsed by twin
black pupils, sex / And business"). His gravitational pull is resisted

by wit. ("When he died / There were already several chilled wives / In sable orbit") The link of father with sun is taken up glancingly later on. In the sleeping mother's bedroom "Blinds beat sun from the bed." The room is held in hushed reserve for the invading child and "red, satyr-thighed / Michael, the Irish setter."

What has been kept apart in detached and taboo encounters falls together at last in the fifth sonnet. There the son is both victim and secret sharer of his parents' lives. In one instant he seems miniaturized, unmanned, a toy soldier melting in a pliable and eternal childhood. At another instant he holds the parents in dated and envied perspective. In a third light he is the capable poet, with them in a lengthening landscape and sharing the self-knowledge of their casual frank exchange:

> It's the fall
> Of 1931. They love each other still.
>
> She: Charlie, I can't stand the pace.
> He: Come on, honey—why you'll bury us all!

Behind the ordinary blunt incompatibility of what they say are shadows already introduced into the poem: his hurrying ambitions, her survivor's protests ("Father Time and Mother Earth, / A marriage on the rocks"). I also hear another echo, which places the scene in a long perspective of repeated follies, worldly callousness and pressured lives. Proust's Duke and Duchess de Guermantes are late for a dinner party. There is time for the Duchess to turn back and change her black shoes for red ones that match her gown, but no time to absorb their friend Swann's news that he has only a few months to live. The Duke's voice drifts cheerily across to the retreating figures of Swann and Marcel: "You're strong as the Pont Neuf. You'll live to bury us all."

"The Broken Home" ends with the home itself, its detailed memory present, but the "real" home receding into the past:

> The real house became a boarding-school.
> Under the ballroom ceiling's allegory
> Someone at last may actually be allowed

> To learn something; or, from my window, cool
> With the unstiflement of the entire story,
> Watch a red setter stretch and sink in cloud.

It takes a moment to realize that the sense of release at the end, "the unstiflement of the entire story," is hypothetical ("Someone at last *may* actually be allowed . . ."). The relief accords so well with our feeling of what the poem has accomplished and our sense that in the puns of the final lines Merrill is at last disengaging himself. The window cools. The satyr-thighed dog, now almost a dream, merges through a play on words with the setting sun, erotic associations subsumed in the pun. There is probably a play on "story" as well, which along with the audacious "red setter" signals that words can accomplish such changes in landscape and feeling that they connect us to a larger planetary orbit—fathers and "suns" and the deep erotic doom of marriages under the sign of Father Time and Mother Earth.

It may be a common—and mistrusted—device of poetic closure, Merrill's calling attention to the poet's role at the end of the poem. But in *Nights and Days*—and especially in the long major poems, "The Thousand and Second Night" and "From the Cupola"—attention to writing coincides with the notion of a house, a dwelling place, a point of repair at a particular moment, the desk, the typewriter. It is as if these poems fulfilled the promise of "An Urban Convalescence"—"To make some kind of house / Out of the life lived, out of the love spent." The conventional ending seems, as in Proust, newly discovered, a psychological necessity.

The very title of this volume refers to the interpenetration and inseparability of the days of raw experience and the nights of imaginative absorption and recall. It is in those late night moments that the poems discover the poet at his desk and perform the ritual separations of poet from his poem. Such episodes, though they occur elsewhere in Merrill's work, seem to have their authentic emotional center in *Nights and Days*. The close of "The

Thousand and Second Night" was almost an emblem of what poetry had come to mean for Merrill. Scheherazade survives by telling her nightly tales, but yearns for "that cold fountain which the flesh / Knows not." The bondage and the pleasure of her stories are expressed in her marriage to the Sultan, the daytime spirit whose joys lie "along that stony path the senses pave." It is he to whom things happen, she who "embroiders" what they mean. In the tenderness of their addresses to one another, the book lays its true and inner counterpoise to the deadlocked male and female voices of "The Broken Home" and to the guilty son of "Childlessness."

> And when the long adventure reached its end,
> I saw the Sultan in a glass, grown old,
> While she, his fair wife still, her tales all told,
> Smiled at him fondly. "O my dearest friend,"
>
> Said she, "and lord and master from the first,
> Release me now. Your servant would refresh
> Her soul in that cold fountain which the flesh
> Knows not. Grant this, for I am faint with thirst."
>
> And he: "But it is I who am your slave.
> Free me, I pray, to go in search of joys
> Unembroidered by your high, soft voice,
> Along that stony path the senses pave."
>
> They wept, then tenderly embraced and went
> Their ways. She and her fictions soon were one.
> He slept through moonset, woke in blinding sun,
> Too late to question what the tale had meant.

The almost eternal twinning of the Sultan and Scheherazade is one of the ways Merrill has of showing how memory and auto-biography ("real life") serve poetry's power to reveal the myths we live by. ("Joyce teaches us to immerse the mythical elements in a well-known setting; Cocteau teaches us to immerse them in a contemporary spoken idiom.") The final desire of the Sultan and Scheherazade to be apart answers to another kind of understanding in *Nights and Days*. The poet alone in his study (in "From the Cupola") sees in his typewriter carriage a "shrunken amphitheater . . . to moon / Hugely above." There is always the danger of being merely elegiac about experience, of "smelling of the lamp." Having gained his equilibrium in the method of memory in *Nights and Days*, he seems ready to throw it all aside in *The Fire Screen*, the strange off-key book he was to publish three years later.

4

It would be interesting to know at what point Merrill saw a larger pattern emerging in his work—the point at which conscious shaping caught up with what unplanned or unconscious experience had thrown his way. In retrospect a reader can see that *Braving the Elements* (1972) gathers behind it the titles—with full metaphorical force—of Merrill's previous books. In *The Country of a Thousand Years of Peace*, *Water Street*, *Nights and Days* and *The Fire Screen*, he had referred to the four elements braved in the book which followed them. (*Divine Comedies* extends it one realm further.) The books do present experience under different aspects, almost as under different zodiacal signs. And *The Fire Screen* is, among other things—and preeminently—the book of love. It reads like a sonnet sequence following the curve of a love affair to its close. Like important sonnet sequences, the implied narrative calls into play a range of anxieties not strictly connected to love, in Merrill's case challenging some of the balanced views of *Nights and Days*.

"The Friend of the Fourth Decade" is the launching point for this book—the poet at forty, setting one part of himself in dialogue with another. What is being tested here is the whole commitment to memory, to personal history, to a house and settling down—the very material to which Merrill entrusted himself after *Water Street*. The "friend" is an alter ego who comes to visit—really to confront—his poet-host, after a long absence. In the opening scene, against the settled atmosphere of his host's house, the friend is shot through with the setting sun so that he appears to be "Any-

man with ears aglow, / . . . gazing inward, mute." The temptation the friend represents is crystallized in a dream at the close of
the poem. "Behind a door marked DANGER . . ."

> Swaddlings of his whole civilization,
> Prayers, accounts, long priceless scroll,
>
> Whip, hawk, prow, queen, down to some last
> Lost comedy, all that fine writing
>
> Rigid with rains and suns,
> Are being gingerly unwound.
>
> There. Now the mirror. Feel the patient's heart
> Pounding—oh please, this once—
>
> Till nothing moves but to a drum.
> See his eyes darken in bewilderment—
>
> No, in joy—and his lips part
> To greet the perfect stranger.

The friend has taught him a mesmerizing game in which
saved-up postcards, a whole history of personal attachments, are
soaked while the ink dissolves. The views remain, but the messages
disappear, "rinsed of the word." When the poet tries it himself,
watching his mother's "Dearest Son" unfurl in the water, the mes-
sage remains legible. "The memories it stirred did not elude me."

"The Friend of the Fourth Decade" tests a dream of escape, a
drama extended and detailed by the poems set in Greece which
follow it in *The Fire Screen*. In some sense the book is like Elizabeth Bishop's *Questions of Travel*, a deepening encounter with another language and a more elemental culture, in which the speaker
becomes, from poem to poem, more identified with his new world,
cleansed of the assumptions of the old. In "To My Greek," the
Greek language, encountered as if it were a demon lover, or a
siren, becomes a radiant, concrete release from the subtleties of the
"mother tongue" and the burden of "Latin's rusted treasure." A

newcomer to Greek, he is forced to be simple, even silly. With Merrill the experience is characteristically amplified. He treats it as a temptation to become "rinsed of the word" and to humble himself speechless in the presence of "the perfect stranger." Both the transcendental and the self-destructive overtones of that phrase from "The Friend of the Fourth Decade," where the "perfect stranger" is also Death, haunt this book.

The initiation into Greece is inseparable from the exhilaration and the mystery of a love affair. It was anticipated in "Days of 1964," the wonderful Cavafid conclusion to *Nights and Days*, and is allowed to run its course in *The Fire Screen*. In "The Envoys" Merrill finds a series of emblems for the sense of adventure and risk experienced in the lover's presence. In three narrative panels, he introduces creatures the lover momentarily traps and tames, binds and then frees: a scurrying lizard, a frightened kitten and a beetle threaded and whirled around his head:

> You knotted the frail harness, spoke,
> Revolved. Eureka! Round your head
> Whirred a living emerald satellite.

The experience is absorbed as a "modulation into a brighter key / Of terror we survive to play."

> Teach me, lizard, kitten, scarabee—
> Gemmed coffer opening on the dram
> Of everlasting life he represents,
>
> His brittle pharoahs in the vale of Hence
> Will hear who you are, who I am,
> And how you bound him close and set him free.

What he shares with the creatures is a moment at the gates of some other world, not insisted on, but imagined as if he were enjoying the danger. All the Greek poems, not only the love poems, benefit from that expansion of feeling. In a dramatic monologue whose tripping couplets are meant to suggest the energetic sing-song of a simple Greek speaker, "Kostas Tympakianakis," Merrill seems almost literally to take up the speaker's invitation: "You'll see a different cosmos through the eyes of a Greek." He adopts the violence, the pride, the clear-eyed tone of the Greek. He accepts the welcome challenge, "Use my name," slips on the offered identity, but registers the gap between them in Kostas's final line: "Who could have imagined such a life as mine?" It is a small but telling rebuke of the poet's imagination always ticking away, its pressures momentarily relieved by taking on the voice of another. *The Fire Screen* contains several poems given over to the pleasures of evoking particular figures, humble like Kostas or sophisticated like Maria, the "muse of my off-days." It sees Greek peasant life through others' eyes ("David's Night at Veliès") or addresses itself to shared moments of happiness, as in "16.ix.65," with "evening's four and twenty candles" and the four friends who return from the beach "with honey on our drunken feet."

But at the core of the Greek section of this book are the love poems, some of them full of lyric intensity, others sharp and painful, like the dramatic soliloquy or fragment "Part of the Vigil," which is, in a sense, the turning point of the affair, a surreal exploration of the images in the lover's heart:

> What
> If all you knew of me were down there, leaking
> Fluids at once abubble, pierced by fierce
> Impulsions of unfeeling, life, limb turning
> To burning cubes, to devil's dice, to ash—
> What if my effigy were down there? What,
> Dear god, if it were not!
> If it were nowhere in your heart!
> Here I turned back.

The lover's image is to "Blaze on" in the poet's own "saved skin." But the poems which follow register both the end of the affair and the folly of thinking of the Greek experience as an escape or oblivion. "Another August," "A Fever" and "Flying to Byzantium" are among the most powerful poems in the book. With "Mornings in a New House," as he imagines a dwelling half-

way back toward cooler American landscapes, the whole experience modulates into a new key, absorbed, retrospective, fading into
myth.

It is appropriate in Merrill's work that recovery should be imagined in terms of a "new house" (or a repainted one in the more
comic and detached version of "After the Fire"). "Mornings in a
New House" has him, "a cold man" who "hardly cares," slowly
brought to life by a fire laid at dawn. Once again the new house is
the available image to set against exposure. "The worst is over,"
the fire a tamed recall of the shattered (or spent?) affair. Against
its "tamed uprush . . . Habit arranges the fire screen." The details of the screen, embroidered by his mother, place the entire
lapsed passion into a withering perspective:

> Crewel-work. His mother as a child
> Stitched giant birds and flowery trees
> To dwarf a house, *her* mother's—see the chimney's
> Puff of dull yarn! Still vaguely chilled,
>
> Guessing how even then her eight
> Years had foreknown him, nursed him, all,
> Sewn his first dress, sung to him, let him fall,
> Howled when his face chipped like a plate,
>
> He stands there wondering until red
> Infraradiance, wave on wave,
> So enters each plume-petal's crazy weave,
> Each worsted brick of the homestead,
>
> That once more, deep indoors, blood's drawn,
> The tiny needlewoman cries,
> And to some faintest creaking shut of eyes
> His pleasure and the doll's are one.

It is hard to disentangle the impulses which contribute to this
poem—harder even because the poet has added a footnote taking
some of it back, imagining passion as itself a defense, not a danger,
like the screen of fire that protects Brünnhilde in Wagner's opera.
But, in the poem proper, the fire screen is devised against the damages of love. It bears, in a sense, the whole retrospective power of

his writing, the ability of memory and art to absorb and rearrange experience. What marks this off from earlier moments in Merrill's poetry is the long perspective which the poem opens up, receding past his immediate pain, past his own childhood of "The Broken Home," to his mother who stitched the screen as a device involving *her* mother.

After all the carefully noted impulses in *The Fire Screen* to leave the mother behind—the atempts to rinse away her handwriting in "Friend of the Fourth Decade"; even the efforts to be free of Latin languages, the "mother tongue"—the poet returns to her in a new way. The "new house" of this poem is interwoven with the house his mother had sewn, *her* mother's house, dwarfed by giant birds and flowery trees. The discovery of these entwined destinies "deep indoors" draws blood. There is something like the remorse of "Childlessness" in what happens. The resources of art are seen as self-protective, even vengeful, a miniaturization of human powers, like the moment in the earlier poem when the annihilated village—teeming generations in dwarfed versions—is loaded aboard sampans and set adrift. But in "Mornings in a New House" the experience is without guilt and is shared in its brittle complexity. Waves of warmth and anger carry him inward to an identification with the "tiny needlewoman" mother, to share the childish pleasure and fear which even then would shape her feelings for the child *she* would one day have. With "some faintest creaking shut of eyes" they both become toys in a larger pattern, at once foreshortened and part of their shared, terrifying but ungrudging humanity. I think what is most notable in this poem is that Merrill, however rueful and pained, has emerged from the erotic fire into a newly defined and felt natural perspective—one which becomes visible and palpable at length in many of the poems of his next book, *Braving the Elements*.

5

I have talked about the double action we must watch in Merrill's poems, the way he twins a witty surface with the poet's power to discover the veined patterns of his life. We must pay special attention to his puns and his settings; they open alternative perspectives against which to read the time-bound and random incidents of daily life. In *Braving the Elements* (1972) and *Divine Comedies* (1976), he has become a master of this idiosyncratic method, something one might call—with apologies—symbolic autobiography, Merrill's way of making apparently ordinary detail transparent to deeper configurations.

This is quite clear in "After the Fire" and "Log," which move us from the world of *The Fire Screen* to that of *Braving the Elements*. The brisk narrative of "After the Fire" brings back the Greek housekeeper Kyria Kleo, whom in "Days of 1964" he had seen wearing "the erotic mask / Worn the world over by illusion / To weddings of itself and simple need." Now, in the new key of "After the Fire," the Athens house has been repainted after a mysterious blaze. Under its "quiet sensible light gray," the house hides his old love affairs as it hides those of Kleo and her rumpled son Noti, their erotic escapades buried and part of the past. The mood of *Braving the Elements* is the mood of the opening invocation, "Log": banked flames of passion, burning and diminution, a life "consumed with that which it was nourished by." The muse discovered "After the Fire" is Kleo's mother, the half-crazed crone. In the yiayia's presence, the candles which gutter before old lovers' ghosts are replaced:

> The snuffed-out candle-ends grow tall and shine,
> Dead flames encircle us, which cannot harm,
> The table's spread, she croons, and I
> Am kneeling pressed to her old burning frame.

The comic crone turns before our eyes into a sybilline figure, mistress of the now harmless flames of passionate memory. She is, in a sense, the informing spirit of the book, for what is new about *Braving the Elements* is the way it opens to long—in some cases, geological—perspectives, the kind of prehistoric, penetrating wisdom which dwarfs and absorbs moments of intense present pain.

The book contains, once again, love poems and poems involving the Oedipal trials of childhood. But these familiar sources of anxiety are in *Braving the Elements* transposed to a different key, resolved as by the all-embracing parenthesis of dream.

For example, family triangles make mysterious appearances in "18 West 11th Street," but as part of a poem in which several generations are run through a New York house, almost as in a strip of film. The house is one in which Merrill spent the first years of his childhood. With one of those attempts history makes to try and rival fiction, this was also the house accidentally destroyed in 1970 by Weathermen who were using it as a center for making bombs in the absence of the owners, parents of one of the revolutionaries. Richard Saez, in a penetrating reading of the poem, points to the unlikely and eloquent connection it makes between "Cathy Wilkerson's destruction of her paternal home and James Merrill's pained elegies for his." The parallels, Saez asserts, "are acts of fate as well as their active wills," as poet and radicals enact in their mutually incompatible fashions, but with equal intensity, the conflict of generations. " '18 West 11th Street,' like the House of Thebes, becomes an emblem for some unavoidable matrix of fate which involves both poet and revolutionary."[10] Inescapably linked to one another, the generations are themselves dissolved in the mirrors of the house and the long stretches of time, each generation finding its own means to suffer and to rebel. Saez is right to single out the close of the poem as having a special new power in Merrill's work:

> Forty-odd years gone by,
> Toy blocks. Church bells. Original vacancy.
> O deepening spring.

Saez points out—that "the 'Original vacancy' of the poem's conclusion is not merely the scene of departure from the poet's childhood. It is man's timeless exclusion from his unforgotten home." Yes, but the phrase also looks forward and seems to say "To Let." With the church bells and "toy blocks" the cityscape seems both distanced and renewed. Of course, the toy blocks are also the children's devices against their parents, whether as poems or explosives. And they are assumed into the ongoing beauty of the exclamation "O deepening spring." Here Saez is particularly acute: "In the concluding tercet nature itself is deflected from its amoral cyclical course to be glazed—not with the gilding, yellowing dust of earlier and lesser achieved poems but—with a patina of human destiny."

That same sense of unfolding destiny informs "Up and Down," a poem whose ingredients are familiar in Merrill's work, but never in so rich a combination. In an earlier book this might well have been two separate poems: one, "Snow King Chair Lift," reflecting the brief exhilarating rising arc of a love affair; the other, "The Emerald," an extraordinary and sympathetic encounter with his mother. But one thing Merrill does in his work is move toward larger and larger units of composition, not only long poems, but combinations of different forms, like the free juxtapositions of prose and more or less formal verse units in "The Thousand and Second Night" and "From the Cupola." The two sections of "Up and Down" limn out, together, an emotional landscape which neither of them could singly suggest.

On the surface it is a poem of contrasts: rising in a ski lift with a lover, descending into a bank vault with the mother; the ostensible freedom of one experience, while in the other, "palatial bronze gates shut like jaws." Yet the exhilaration of the ski lift—it begins in dramatic present tenses—is what is relegated finally to a cherished snapshot and to the past tense: "We gazed our little fills at boundlessness." The line almost bursts with its contradictions: unslaked appetite, or appetite only fulfilled and teased by "gazing our little fills." The lovers have not quite reached the condition of the Shakespearean "pitiful thrivers in their gazing spent"; they are more buoyant, but with a redirected and only momentary pleasure. "The Emerald," on the other hand, begins in brisk easy narrative pasts and moves toward a moment in the very present which the ski-lift section had forsaken. More important, whatever the surface contrasts between the two sections, there is an irresistible connection between the discoveries made by each. Or rather, the feelings of the opening poem enable the son to understand what happens to the mother in the closing poem. In the vault an unexpected secret jumps to light:

> Rustle of tissue, a sprung
> Lid. Her face gone queerly lit, fair, young,
> Like faces of our dear ones who have died.
>
> No rhinestone now, no dilute amethyst,
> But of the first water, linking star to pang,
> Teardrop to fire, my father's kisses hang
> In lipless concentration round her wrist.

The effect resembles the moment of thunder and lightning on the chair-lift in Part I, but here things are seen in a prolonged transforming light, the queer deathlike glow when the "mud-brown" coffin of a box is opened. It is as if the glimpse of "boundlessness" in Part I can only be extended and refined in the eternal light of underground. The poet and his mother are seen as part of a performance in the "green room" which the emerald suggests. Before his eyes she grows both youthful and like the dead. Surviving two husbands, she can still be transfixed by memory, transformed by the bracelet. "My father's kisses hang / In lipless concentration round her wrist." Contraries are reconciled: "star to pang, / Teardrop to fire." She is bride, widow and mother all at once, and something like the eternally preserved Mesopotamian consorts, "girl-bride jewelled in his grave."

Against this background mother and son have the unspoken reconciliation discussed earlier in this chapter. He slips onto her finger the emerald she had intended for his bride, the very ring his father gave her when the poet was born. All these elements compose an increasingly luminous frieze: "The world beneath the world is brightening." It is one of those moments assumed, as many are in *Braving the Elements*, into an ongoing process of time, and experienced not elegiacally but with a sense of promise.

That deepening emotional landscape is most strongly suggested in the new physical surroundings of *Braving the Elements*. A series of difficult poems takes place in the Far West. Pieces like "Under Libra" and "In Nine Sleep Valley" are love poems played out against dwarfing panoramas and the geological erosions of a non-human world.

> Geode, the troll's melon
> Rind of crystals velvet smoke meat blue
> Formed far away under fantastic
> Pressures, then cloven in two
> By the taciturn rock shop man, twins now forever
>
> Will they hunger for each other
> When one goes north and one goes east?
>
> I expect minerals never do,
> Enough for them was a feast
> Of flaws, the molten start and glacial sleep,
> The parting kiss.
>
> Still face to face in halfmoonlight
> Sparkling comes easy to the Gemini.
>
> Centimeters deep yawns the abyss.

In "Under Libra" ancient stones are introduced into the poet's house ostensibly as doorstops and paperweights, but really as reminders of another scale of living. He goes "in the small hours from room to room / Stumbling onto their drugged stubborn sleep." These talismans overshadow desire; they place it in a perspective where past and future edge out the present. The solid human protagonists of the poem are disssolved before our eyes:

> . . . ten years from next morning, pen in hand,
>
> Looking through saltwater, through flames,
> Enkindlings of an absent *I* and *you*,
> Live, spitting pronouns, sparks that flew

And were translated into windiest
Esperanto, zero tongue of powers
Diplomatic around 1 a.m.'s

Undripping centerpiece, the Swan . . .
Days were coming when the real thing
No longer shrugged a wing.

Some of the poems are pure ventriloquism. "The Black Mesa"
speaks; so do "Banks of a Stream Where Creatures Bathe." They
seem to embody a consensus of human voices, mythically inured
to experience. History, the details of private lives—everything repeats itself in the long views these poems take. Hearing the poet
take on these roles is like talking to survivors. "The Black Mesa,"
addressing the low flatland, musters for a moment the tone of an
eager roué, but finally lapses back into a weary geological view of
his experience, outwaiting all competitors and invaders: "I steal
past him who next reclaims you, keep / Our hushed appointments,
grain by grain . . . / Dust of my dust, when will it all be plain?"
The effect is to make expressions of human tenderness mere instances of the larger erosions and destinies which outlast them.

"Syrinx" is the most successful of such poems. She is, of course,
an established mythological figure, brightly familiar from Marvell:
"And Pan did after Syrinx speed / Not as a nymph, but for a reed."
Merrill takes up her fragile link to the nature from which she was
abstracted, "a thinking reed." Just who is she in this version? She
addresses the poet as if she were his muse and his lover. She is
sophisticated enough to know about slipware and to quote Pascal;
also, to make puns about fashion and the Pan-pipe's traditional
shape: "Among the wreckage, bent in Christian weeds, / Illiterate—X my mark—I tremble, still / A thinking reed."

"Bent in Christian weeds" makes it sound as if she were used to
dresses by Chanel, and "Illiterate—X my mark" walks a tightrope
of ingenuity and feeling. As unlikely as her witty denial of literacy
may be, Syrinx keeps shucking off the claims of words as if they
were merely garments. The most outrageous example is the incor-

poration of the musical scale: "Who puts his mouth to me / Draws out the scale of love and dread— / O ramify, sole antidote!" The musician's breath or the lover's kiss, and then the high tragedienne's apostrophe, which, on a second glance, taking in the enjambment ("d— / O"), we see disintegrate magically into the musical scale. This is precisely the action the poem repeats over and over: a human gesture, then the witty afflatus and effort of words which slip back before our eyes into analytic formulas, the do-re-mi of the scale, or the particles of a mathematical formula which expresses metastasis. Syrinx seems caught between human demands and ingenuity, which make her "tremble, still" and, on the other hand, her sense of being a worn part of a growing and disintegrating world:

> Foxglove
> Each year, cloud, hornet, fatal growths
>
> Proliferating by metastasis
> Rooted their total in the gliding stream.

Over and over the cleverness of the poem is matched by a hypnotic natural intonation, no more than in the astonishing close; as Syrinx slides back into her "scarred case,"

> Whose silvery breath-tarnished tones
> No longer rivet bone and star in place
>
> Or keep from shriveling, leather round a stone,
> The sunbather's precocious apricot
>
> Or stop the four winds racing overhead
>   Nought
>   Waste   Eased
>   Sought

Those last four words clothe the cardinal points in notions of human aspiration and loss, which we may understand in varying combinations and intensities, depending on the order in which we read them. But ultimately they slip back into the toneless ideogram of the ongoing winds. How odd human words and feelings seem, depicted in this particular way. The lozenge of four words is tinged by, but ultimately surpasses, individual feelings.

6

No matter how much *Braving the Elements* attunes us to Merrill's desire for longer landscapes, nothing he had done could have prepared for the deep focus of "The Book of Ephraim," the long poem which makes up two-thirds of Merrill's *Divine Comedies*. The poem stands in something of the same relation to Merrill's work as *History* does to Lowell's—a massed, retrospective piece written at the height of the poet's career. Both works come to grips with the presence of the dead, though in entirely contrasting ways. The long threatening wreckage of Lowell's "history" spurs him into precarious, self-assertive positions. The eroded constantly changing world of "The Book of Ephraim," on the contrary, seems ultimately a nourishing one for James Merrill.

Short of the extended analysis which "The Book of Ephraim" invites and for which this chapter is not the proper occasion, there are still ways to talk about the vital light the poem sheds on Merrill's unfolding autobiography. We might begin, for example, with "M"—almost the exact center of the poem's twenty-six alphabetical sections. (It repeats the arc of letters on the Ouija board, one of its "sources.") "M" recounts a blissful dream of Merrill's friend Maya Deren, a maker of experimental films. The telling is blithe and entertaining but the story is also a paradigm, an *ars poetica* for Merrill's work. Maya dreams that she is at a glittering reception. She alone is in black mourning dress, but a youthful admirer, in whose eyes she too turns young again, leads her to a spring in which everything, as in a negative, is transformed. Her black garb, veil and jewels become sparkling white, her pale skin black, "a not yet / Printed self." Then she must part from the admirer, whom she will rejoin only after "long trials."

> Dream? She wakes from it in bliss.
>
> So what does that turn out to mean?
> Well, Maya has lately moved to the top floor

Of a brownstone whence, a hundred and six years
Ago, a lady more or less her age
Passed respectably to the First Stage.
Now (explains Ephraim) in a case like this
At least a century goes by before
One night comes when the soul, revisiting
Its deathplace here below, locates and enters
On the spot a sleeping form its own
Age and sex (easier said than done
In rural or depopulated areas:
E treats us here to the hilarious
Upshot of a Sioux brave's having chosen
By mistake a hibernating bear).
Masked in that sleeping person, then, the soul
For a few outwardly uneventful hours—
Position shifting, pillowcrease, a night
Of faint sounds, gleams, moonset, mosquito bite—
Severs what LAST THREADS bind it to the world.
Meanwhile (here comes the interesting bit)
The sleeper's soul, dislodged, replaces it
In Heaven.

                          . . . .
This dream . . . is a low-budget
Remake—imagine—of the *Paradiso*.
Not otherwise its poet toured the spheres
While Someone very highly placed up there,
Donning his bonnet, in and out through that
Now famous nose haled the cool Tuscan night.
The resulting masterpiece takes years to write;
More, since the dogma of its day
Calls for a Purgatory, for a Hell,
Both of which Dante thereupon, from footage
Too dim or private to expose, invents.
His Heaven, though, as one cannot but sense,
Tercet by tercet, is pure Show and Tell.

This fable, offered by Ephraim, the entertaining familiar spirit of Merrill's Ouija board, is naturally an attractive one for the poet. We recall his *First Poems*, their desire to escape to a projected ideal world. Later in his career he turns to the everyday, to wit, to an accomplished social tone and to narrative. But always with the sense that the world discerned is not quite real, that in its

flashing action he might catch glimpses of patterns activated by
the charged details of his life. Maya's dream and the attendant
fable of Dante appeal to him precisely because they capture the
allure of poetry, its use of worldliness to regain access to an invisible world.

What the young Merrill could not have foreseen was that the
future ideal world he was working toward was not an empty evacu-
ated space, but instead a rich experience of *déjà vû*. For him it
was to be full of the past, of luminous figures, the living and the
dead, all of whom coexist in "The Book of Ephraim" by virtue of
the attention Merrill has given them throughout his work and the
value he has come to attach to them. The book includes figures
resonant from other, earlier poems: his mother, his father, Hans
Lodeizen (from *The Country of a Thousand Years of Peace*), the
Greek Strato, David Jackson, Maisie the cat, Kyria Kleo, as well
as literary masters like Wallace Stevens and W. H. Auden.

Readers will take to Ephraim's revealed system of reincarnations
and heavenly patronage with varying degrees of belief and astonishment, just as they will accept as literal or metaphorical, according to temperament, its dramatic occasion: "The Book of a
Thousand and One Evenings Spent / With David Jackson at the
Ouija Board / In Touch with Ephraim Our Familiar Spirit." But
what is immediately available to readers is the way this poem allows Merrill to think of the past as nourishing—and without the
sense of elegy which marks Lowell's *History*. Ephraim speaks to
the narrator (section Q) of a community "WITHIN SIGHT OF & ALL
CONNECTED TO EACH OTHER DEAD OR ALIVE   NOW DO U UNDERSTAND
WHAT HEAVEN IS   IT IS THE SURROUND OF THE LIVING". Of these figures he says "IT IS EASY TO CALL THEM BRING THEM AS FIRES WITHIN
SIGHT OF EACH OTHER ON HILLS". Metaphorically speaking, it is the
kind of writing Merrill has done which makes many of these figures, finally, so innocently available to him, part of a network of
affinities. "The Book of Ephraim" bears witness to a lifetime of
continuing attention to and care for figures who have become
resonant in his memory.

This poem, for example, returns with feeling ease to the memories of his father and his father's death—all the more remarkable when one thinks of Merrill's gallery of reactions to his father, running the gamut from satire in "The Broken Home" and in his novel *The Seraglio* to the guilt reflected in "Childlessness." In "The Book of Ephraim" they are spunky affectionate equals in the plenum of birth and decay. The freedom that vision allows bears fruit in "Yánnina," one of the independent shorter poems in *Divine Comedies*. Helen Vendler is right to speak of it as "a remarkable joining of filial and paternal spheres." After a visit to Yánnina, capital of the last Turkish potentate in Greece, Ali Pasha, Merrill draws a portrait of the old despot, of the two women most notably attached to him—one a spiritual, one a fleshly love—and of the conflated gore and charm of Ali's life. What comes to matter in the poem is the intricate interweaving of present and past. Toward the end he links Ali's dual nature with his (Merrill's) own father's. More important all along, in a dialogue with a younger companion, he has been testing contradictions in his own nature which subtly identify him with the two vanished "fathers" in the "brave old world" of the poem.

"Yánnina" is a tribute to the sifting, amassing and reconciling powers of memory. It shows how the attitudes behind "The Book of Ephraim" help to refigure individual experience under the elongating pressures of time. Within "The Book of Ephraim" Merrill was to acknowledge a new sense of his rapport with Proust. He recalls in section T the climactic episode when Proust's narrator revisits "society"—an afternoon party—after an absence of years. For a moment Marcel mistakes the aging characters for bewigged figures at an eighteenth-century masquerade.

> Too violent,
> I once thought, that foreshortening in Proust—
> A world abruptly old, whitehaired, a reader
> Looking up in puzzlement to fathom
> Whether ten years or forty have gone by.
> Young, I mistook it for an unconvincing

> Trick of the teller. It was truth instead
> Babbling through his own astonishment.

The system of patrons and representatives, reincarnations and respites from earthly life which Ephraim reveals to our protagonists, JM and DJ, is, in one sense, a counterweight to the shock of aging. Or is it an anticipation of and response to the personal erosions to which this poem also bears witness? Among the many possible readings of this poem, one certainly grows out of the fact that Ephraim and his transcendental system result from the loving collaboration of JM and DJ. His visits begin with the second summer of their joint tenancy in Stonington, the same tenancy welcomed in *Water Street* as a change of life and poetic direction.

From the very start the tone Ephraim takes with his two "pupils" is one of engaging worldliness, as in "E":

> TAKE our teacher told us
> FROM SENSUAL PLEASURE ONLY WHAT WILL NOT
> DURING IT BE EVEN PARTLY SPOILED
> BY FEAR OF LOSING TOO MUCH

A psychiatrist, consulted in a period when the two mediums have suffered a short-circuit with their board, takes a flatter view of things (section I):

> "There's a phrase
> You may have heard—what you and David do
> We call folie à deux.
> Harmless; but can you find no simpler ways
>
> To sound each other's depths of spirit
> Than taking literally that epigram
> Of Wilde's I'm getting damn
> Tired of hearing my best patients parrot?"

The patient JM is forced through the hoops of "Given a mask . . . we'll tell . . . *the* truth." The doctor also presses JM to another explanation of "these odd / Inseminations by psycho-roulette":

> I stared, then saw the light:
> "Somewhere a Father Figure shakes his rod

> At sons who have not sired a child?
> Through our own spirit we can both proclaim
> And shuffle off the blame
> For how we live—that good enough?"

"I've heard worse," says the shrink.

But the poem provides more refined explanations. Ephraim tells them (section G) that JM is fortunate to be in his last life while DJ is sentenced to further sessions on earth. They protest being separated: they live together, E. is insensitive. Then a pregnant pause.

> His answer's unrecorded. The cloud passed
> More quickly than the shade it cast,
>
> Foreshadower of nothing, dearest heart,
> But the dim wish of lives to drift apart.

The poem is fully responsive to such nuances of feeling: the separations of DJ and JM; their returns to the house; physical changes; deteriorations in the house itself; the twilight comedies of DJ's aged parents; the less and less frequent meetings with DJ over the Ouija board. These insights help make the poem emotionally convincing and various. If the poem reaps the rewards and transfusions of memory, at every stage of the game, accompanying the triumphs, it gives a sense of the intimacies taken and foregone.

So, near the end (section Y):

> And here was I, or what was left of me.
> Feared and rejoiced in, chafed against, held cheap,
> A strangeness that was us, and was not, had
> All the same allowed for its description,
> And so brought at least me these spells of odd,
> Self-effacing balance.

The lines acknowledge an almost involuntary access to another world ("A strangeness . . . had . . . allowed for its description"). The strangeness "was us, and was not." In that phrase and in other contradictions ("Feared and rejoiced in, chafed against, held cheap") Merrill concentrates the struggles of this poem. The life shared with DJ—and the houses shared with him in Athens and in Stonington—is revealed and valued in "The Book of Ephraim" as the ground bass of Merrill's poetry since *Water Street*. "The Book of Ephraim" is almost a recapitulation of the themes of his work during that time, and draws many of its principal characters back onstage. The Stonington house in particular, with its domed room and its stardeck, had been conjured up again and again for figures as luminous (and diverse) as Maisie (the cat) and Psyche (the heroine of "From the Cupola") before it was revealed as a home for Ephraim as well. This imaginative refiguring is an example of a style Richard Poirier sees as particularly American and particularly exposed: "images of housing, of possession, and of achieving by relinquishment of one's inheritance some original relation to time and space."[11] The activity of "The Book of Ephraim" is finally one in which Merrill achieves some "original relation to time and space" and one in which the sense of relinquishment is sharp and full. It is precisely at the moments when writing penetrates memory and the familiar domestic scene that Merrill is most aware of depletion: "What was left of me." The house at the end of the poem seems cold and empty. A mysterious and unidentified thief has been and gone. The two communicants are on the verge of burning the "letters," transcripts of their sessions with Ephraim. Writing the poem—making Ephraim's panorama his own—has brought Merrill to the point where he feels he has to withdraw. "Let's be downstairs, leave all this, put the light out." The end of the poem is deliberately muted, using neutral domestic gestures to cover a certain fear about the light his imagination has cast. The quoted sentence is meant to sound more like whistling in the dark than like a buried echo of a resolute Othello.

"The Book of Ephraim" is a compendium of voices—individual and social, emulated, sometimes feared and discarded. It suggests ways in which the apparently random material of our lives and

reading, history, gossip—the rational and irrational bombard-
ments—are somehow absorbed and selected for our experience.
Echoes and re-echoes tease us with patterns whose existence we
suspected but whose details were not yet clear. With its eddies
and turns, its combination of tones, its range of high talk and low,
"The Book of Ephraim" suggests how such patterns gather in a
human life and assume the force of conviction. Merrill also suggests the price we pay for that knowledge.

It is possible to see how "The Book of Ephraim" enabled Merrill to write the very special kinds of shorter poems which make up
the opening section of *Divine Comedies*. Having written as much
as he did about his life, having circled and recircled key figures
and scenes, he had amassed a large repertory of analogous experiences, moments so resembling each other that each begins to provide a context for the other. "Lost in Translation" reaps the rewards of that kind of attention. It begins with the apparently
random way things happen to us and it includes a number of
episodes not explicitly related. The central story, interleaved with
others, is that of a child separated from his parents for the summer.
He lives with his governess, a French Mademoiselle, and they are
eagerly awaiting a jigsaw puzzle which, in the course of the narrative, is assembled and then its pieces dispersed. The poem weaves
connections between the world of the child, vividly recalled in the
present tense, and that of the remembering adult, who only makes
his full entrance in the past tenses of the long rhapsodic coda.[12]
(Even a more recent episode—a mind-reader in London—is told as
if the child were perceiving it: "This grown man reenters, wearing
grey.") An odd massing of consciousness takes place. At first the
poet speaks distantly of "the child," "the boy"; it isn't until mid-
way through the poem that the child's experience so recaptures
him as to identify it in the first person, his very self: "*Puzzle begun
I write.*"

For the child the only puzzle is the literal one, the jigsaw. The
events of his life have a magical authenticity for him—the devotion
of Mademoiselle; the wonderful assembly of the puzzle which

represents an Oriental scene; even a numinous quality in the individual pieces, their discrete shapes unrelated to the eventual content. He is infatuated with what seems to be an ostrich, a witch on a broomstick, an hourglass, all of which are to vanish into the Eastern narrative.

Other puzzles are only identified later, and by the adults, as puzzles: why he spends the summer without parents; Mademoiselle's secret history, her mélange of French and German, which he only thinks about much later in the midst of another puzzle—reading Valéry and recalling, but unable to find, a Rilke translation of the poem "Palme." One tug at memory seems to have brought a whole knot of memories to the surface. Or is his reaction triggered by the Valéry poem itself—the fable of the tree with its roots drinking springs below the desert, which the French poet compared to the seemingly pointless days which mysteriously nourish our lives? ("That sunlit paradigm whereby the tree / Taps a sweet wellspring of authority," Merrill says.)

All these experiences are felt, without anxiety, as analogous: Mademoiselle's secret, the lost Rilke translation, the Valéry poem, the excitement of putting together the puzzle, the feel of the summer without parents. The sense of mysterious relations is crystallized for us when the puzzle, as if by magic (and in the only regular stanzas of the poem, the Rubaiyat stanza Merrill likes so much), gathers before our eyes: "Lo! it assembles on the shrinking Green." A fable emerges: grandly confronting one another, a Sheik and a veiled woman, who appear to be quarrelling, like Oberon and Titania, over a young boy, a page. The scene is captured in the manner fairy tales use; according to Bruno Bettelheim, the enchantment transfigures the violent and critical passages of life. Only below the surface do we feel the stronger implications of the completed puzzle, "Eternal Triangle, Great Pyramid!" and its relevance to the child's own abandoned and perhaps disputed state.

What is interesting about this particular version of "The Broken Home" is that it is absorbed into a larger constellation of analogies whose model is "translation." The poem returns at the end to translation, to Valéry's poem and Rilke's version, to the sense of what is foregone and what is gained, and to the conviction that nothing is "lost" in translation, or that "All is translation / And every bit of us is lost in it." Merrill, unable to find the Rilke version, still feels he *knows*

> How much of the sun-ripe original
> Felicity Rilke made himself forego
> (Who loved French words—verger, mûr, parfumer)
> In order to render its underlying sense.
> Know already in that tongue of his
> What Pains, what monolithic Truths
> Shadow stanza to stanza's symmetrical
> Rhyme-rutted pavement. Know that ground plan left
> Sublime and barren, where the warm Romance
> Stone by stone faded, cooled; the fluted nouns
> Made taller, lonelier than life
> By leaf-carved capitals in the afterglow.
> The owlet umlaut peeps and hoots
> Above the open vowel. And after rain
> A deep reverberation fills with stars.

In his own absorption of Rilke's Valéry, Merrill performs the process acted out so many times in the poem. After the "warm Romance," after the enchanting childhood, he is left with the adult conviction or realization of a "ground plan left / Sublime and barren," the pattern discovered and echoed in unexpected corners of 'his life, "color of context," what might have seemed waste transmuted to "shade and fiber, milk and memory."

Divine Comedies represents a use of Proust that the author of *Water Street* might never have foreseen, as the Oedipal dramas and attachment to any single house fade into a deeper set of landmarks. In the shorter poems of this book Merrill plays many different—and for him—new roles, sees himself in new relations (son and godfather, inheritor and the man who makes his will). Finally in "The Book of Ephraim" he becomes part of a strange landscape of the living and the dead, luminous and life-giving. He responds to it with the astonishment Proust recorded in *Le Temps Re-*

trouvé, when the narrator speaks of a book which would substitute a plot based on the sensations of the author's very life, foregoing invention and make-believe:

> The suffering caused him by others, his attempts to forestall it, the conflicts provoked by his suffering and the other cruel person—all that, interpreted by his intelligence, might furnish the material for a book not only as fine as if it had been imagined and invented, but also as completely foreign to the author's reveries as if he had been absorbed in himself and happy, as surprising to him and as much the product of chance as an accidental caprice of the imagination.[13]

It is precisely Merrill's surprise at his enlarged, nourished and idio-syncratic relation to his past which *Divine Comedies* records.

IV ADRIENNE RICH
Face to Face

> I'm naked, ignorant,
> a naked man fleeing
> across the roofs
> who could with a shade of difference
> be sitting in the lamplight
> against the cream wallpaper
> reading—not with indifference—
> about a naked man
> fleeing across the roofs.
>
> "The Roofwalker" 1961

"The Broken Home" is a title James Merrill and Adrienne Rich might have shared. An odd pairing, an "instructive contrast," poets whose audiences certainly do not overlap. As young writers, almost exact contemporaries, from good colleges, and with advanced literary tastes, both Merrill and Rich were precocious and, in their early poems, mannerly and skilled. Merrill's *First Poems* appeared in 1951, the same year in which Rich, still an undergraduate at Radcliffe, had her first book, *A Change of World*, selected by W. H. Auden for the Yale Series of Younger Poets.

It takes about fifteen years of hard work, as Jonathan Bishop reminds us, for a poet to change the style of a coterie or period into an individual dialect. Both Merrill and Rich—in their very different ways—have accomplished that change, and both give the impression now of having used poetry to achieve a self, the poet choosing the words he or she lives by. These two poets define, in some ways, opposed attitudes: Merrill, working the shuttle of memory to win his freedom from the past; Rich, working in a jagged present, always pitched toward the future and change. But it is worthwhile, for a moment, to speak of them in the same breath. For they are both that half-generation younger than Robert Lowell which allows them not to be beguiled by the Augustan, public, historical temptation which bedevilled Lowell's imagination.

Both Merrill and Rich are strongly committed to autobiography, to poetry as an instrument of personal resolve and clarification, without sharing any of Lowell's paralysis before the lost connections of American history and of his own New England past. The forceful suggestion in Lowell's poetry is that, in the face of history, no such clarification or resolve is possible; we take our places among the ruins of time.

When I say that "The Broken Home" is a title Merrill and Rich might have shared, I mean that some of the strongest poems each has written give accounts, continually emerging, of conventional family life blasted or transformed, "seen through." Each has pursued in and through writing an identity quite independent of traditional definitions. Each has experienced the fragmentation Lowell talks about—and has taken it as a new beginning. Each has sustained the effort long enough for us to see it as a developed and a developing alternative. Here, the resemblances end—in refusing to shelter in others' homes and defined roles; in writing resolutely out of a sense of charged separations.

One emotional center of Merrill's work, as we have seen, is that of a child of a broken marriage. He returns to it in "Childlessness," "Lost in Translation," "Days of 1935" and, of course, "The Broken Home." The dedication of his work, in "An Urban Convalescence," springs from "the dull need to make some kind of house / Out of the life lived, out of the love spent." Rich, on the other hand, began speaking partly out of a woman's sense of separateness in her marriage. We hear this in poems like "Orion" (1965) in which she yearns to be out in the open with the cold, burning star, "my fierce half-brother," away from indoors and the hearth where "A man reaches behind my eyes / And finds them empty," and where "children are dying my death / and eating crumbs of my life."

Rich herself has given the best critical account of the conflicts out of which that poem grew.

> The poem "Orion" . . . is a poem of reconnection with a part of myself I had felt I was losing—the active principle, the energetic imagination, the "half-brother" whom I projected, as I had for many years, into the constellation Orion. It's no accident that the words "cold and egotistical" appear in this poem, and are applied to myself. The choice still seemed to be between "love"—womanly, maternal love, altruistic love—a love defined and ruled by the weight of an entire culture; and egotism—a force directed by men into creation, achievement, ambition, often at the expense of others, but justifiably so.[1]

That comment comes from an essay called "When We Dead Awaken," which has an equally apt subtitle, "Writing as Re-Vision." Rich was trying, especially in the book called *The Will to Change* (1971), to use poetry in a new way. "A Valediction Forbidding Mourning" (1970) is only the most explicit of the continuing farewells in that book, farewells to an old way of love and an old grammar of loving. "They gave me a drug that slowed the healing of wounds." As if written under that drug and prompted by the desire to forget an old composure, Rich has adopted a new manner in writing about her life.

I want to locate the individuality of her autobiographical style by reading one of her poems alongside one of Robert Lowell's. What should become apparent—and what links her to Merrill and many other poets of her generation—is that Rich and other younger writers are no longer elegiac about history. Lowell *is*; this is part of his legacy from Pound and Eliot. Extremely self-conscious about his role as poet, Lowell can, as Thomas Edwards reminds us, take on "something like the ceremonial role of the caster of auguries." "Lowell's fears about the American present mix with his complex personal attachment to the lost America of his ancestors."[2] He made poetry out of baffled attempts to join the public and private worlds, or, more accurately, out of his sense of public and private ruin. We see him at that task and at his best in "For the Union Dead," a poem I want to juxtapose with Rich's "The Burning of Paper Instead of Children."

"For the Union Dead" (1960) is an attempt, as Rich's poem is, to connect individual feelings with a historical moment and with political attitudes. Lowell's poem shuttles between present and past, a series of comparisons between the Boston of his childhood and Boston in the early 1960s, with steam-shovels eating up the Boston Common to make way for a new parking garage. The emotional center of the poem is an implicit challenge to the present from the past—from the heroic figure of the Bostonian, Colonel Shaw, who died leading an all-black regiment in the Civil War. The parking garage excavations shake the relief St. Gaudens made to honor Shaw and his black infantry. Not only does the poet contrast present and past, but he sets himself in spirit at a distance from both of them. In neither his own present nor in his past does he appear to have the "gentle tautness," the "angry wrenlike vigilance" he admires in Colonel Shaw. To his eyes, "The stone statues of the abstract Union soldier / grow slimmer and younger each year." We see him as spectator in a series of overlapping scenes and in hypnotically parallel positions: first, a childhood memory, his nose pressed against the aquarium glass; then, in the present, against the barbed-wire fence surrounding the Common garage excavations; finally, crouched before a television set watching "the drained faces of Negro school-children." The overlapping images keep teasing him toward connections he can't quite make.

For example, at the aquarium as a child, his hand "tingled / to burst the bubbles / drifting from the noses of the cowed, compliant fish." Now, in front of the television, the school-children's faces "rise like balloons." A moment (and a stanza break) later, "Colonel Shaw / is riding on his bubble" waiting for "the blesséd break." The poet is there mainly to register these parallels, drily, and to suggest historical connections which both he and his readers are too stunned, too baffled to make more clearly. It is not only that contrasts are made between present and past, but that a new order has taken over which devours the past and the powers of the personality to experience it with pleasure. Lowell's ways of talking about his childhood are demystified and vulgarized as the same images are summoned up for a brutalized present. The new cars, replacing the fish of his childhood aquarium, "nose forward like fish; / a savage servility / slides by on grease." It is only Shaw's monument which "sticks like a fishbone / in the city's throat." For the rest, the speaker in his elegiac posture seems robbed of his experience, even of his anger, and reduced to a puzzled reportorial tone.

Rich, talking about her experience, has fears almost the obverse of Lowell's, fears that the past will rob her of her present rather than vice versa. The epigraph of "The Burning of Paper Instead of Children" comes from Fr. Daniel Berrigan on trial in Baltimore: "I was in danger of verbalizing my moral impulses out of existence." The poem is touched off by an incident in which her eleven-year-old son and a neighbor's child have burned a mathematics textbook on the last day of school. The neighbor punishes his son: " 'The burning of a book,' he says, 'arouses terrible sensations in me, memories of Hitler; there are few things that upset me so much as the idea of burning a book.' "

The episode releases a number of charged memories and contradictory feelings, held more or less in solution by the urgent form Rich has chosen for the poem. There are five sections; two predominantly in prose, two in verse and one a mixture. They seem to be five "takes" on a present emotion, accumulating intensity but quite independent of any sense of logical time. Perhaps they are Rich's version of Charles Olson's "field theory" of composition in which the poem represents not so much a series of feelings, logically developed, as a field in which these charged emotions are simultaneously present. For example, the first section tells the triggering anecdote in prose, then moves into a series of verse memories: "Back there: the library, walled / with green Britannicas . . ."

> the crocodiles in Herodotus
> the Book of the Dead
> the *Trial of Jeanne d'Arc*, so blue
> I think, It is her color
>
> and they take the book away
> because I dream of her too often
>
> love and fear in a house
> knowledge of the oppressor
> I know it hurts to burn

A number of conflicting feelings coexist in the passage. Books are nurturing; they appeal to the child even through an affectionate identification of their content with their colors. The books are exotic; they feed her ardor. There is a mixture of gratitude—longing for the library—and resentment against the parents who censored her reading and guarded her from her feelings. What is important is the free-floating language in which these charged contradictions are conveyed. Without punctuation, that last triad of the opening section pulls in different directions. *Knowledge of the oppressor:* knowledge belonging to them, transmitted by them; or knowledge *about* them (she feels them as oppressors). These feelings gather behind "I know it hurts to burn" which has both transitive and intransitive force. It hurt for Joan of Arc to be burned (the child dreams of the martyr too often). It hurts to burn books, though her disagreement with the neighbor who punishes his son qualifies her childhood love of reading. The phrase also refers back to the epigraph and the Berrigan brothers who had burned Selective Service records in protest against the Vietnam War. Perhaps most important, it "hurts to burn" in ardor, indignation and powerlessness, as the speaker of this poem does. She has gathered this battery of conflicting responses and has found an indeterminate sentence (no period—in this case, itself a statement, not a mannerism) which will register the pulls in different directions.

Later in the poem Rich transcribes an urgent paragraph written by an Open Enrollment student:

People suffer highly in poverty and it takes dignity and in-
telligence to overcome this suffering. Some of the suffering
are: a child did not had dinner last night: a child steal be-
cause he did not have money to buy it: to hear a mother say
she do not have money to buy food for her children and to
see a child without cloth it will make tears in your eyes.

(the fracture of order
the repair of speech
to overcome this suffering)

The last three unpunctuated lines leave important questions up in
the air. Do we link the second and third lines, read them together
to imply that the repair of grammar and speech *might* overcome
suffering? Or do the three lines fall separately—three breaths,
phrases testing three thoughts, the last introduced by a floating
infinitive, as if to pose a wondering question or exclamation? (*How*
to overcome this suffering? or *If only* one could overcome . . .)

Rich uses her floating infinitives resourcefully. Another section,
a peaceful sexual encounter, begins "To imagine a time of silence . . ." The sentence is never completed, but the movement
is. No main verb ever gives a logical valence to the infinitive, but
instead we sail directly into the feeling, as if, for a moment, the
poet gets her wish, a fulfilled subjunctive. What is accomplished is

relief

from this tongue   this slab of limestone
or reinforced concrete
fanatics and traders
dumped on this coast   wildgreen   clayred
that breathed once
in signals of smoke
sweep of the wind

knowledge of the oppressor
this is the oppressor's language

yet I need it to talk to you

The knot of words and feelings is hard to untie, and the knotted quality is conveyed long before the speaker makes it explicit with "yet I need it to talk to you." Lineation and spacing help to locate counter-currents. The resentment against language, built up as "tongue," becomes "slab of limestone," spills over into "fanatics and traders." Irritation is then defused in the intense "wildgreen" and "clayred," relished sharp apprehensions of a pristine America, each word isolated, savored, as in a breath of appreciation and pleasure. When the phrase "knowledge of the oppressor" returns as a refrain, it seems overstated—perhaps deliberately, though I think not. Whether intended or not, "knowledge" now carries some of the complex understanding of the previous verse paragraph. Frustration prevails, but some breath of the experienced pleasure remains ("wildgreen   clayred").

"The Burning of Paper . . ." circles around questions of the tyranny of language over feeling. Its strength lies in the way it draws upon many areas of feeling: childhood memories, sexual anger and jealousy, sexual pleasure, political protest, suffering in poverty. A mind so various is itself a challenge to the inflexibility, the historical weight of language. With impatience, the last section of "The Burning of Paper . . ." moves into a fluid prose. "I am composing on the typewriter late at night, thinking of today. How well we all spoke. A language is the map of our failures." The staccato sentences which follow gather up the varying frustrations about language accumulated in the poem—Frederick Douglass, the black abolitionist who had been born a slave, "wrote an English purer than Milton's"; Joan of Arc could not read, spoke a peasant form of French—then follow snatches from the black student's essay on poverty and from her own scene of erotic misunderstanding; finally recall of the Berrigans and of her own anger at her neighbor. Phrases come back urgently: "I cannot touch you now"; "this is the oppressor's language"; "I know it hurts to burn." That last sentence now bristles with its full range of gathered meaning: sexual, political (the Berrigans, the neighbor boy burning a book), historical (Joan of Arc). It carries the charge of anger and frustration at being, as she puts it in another poem, "bombarded" with a whole range of intense and often contradictory feelings. These tell upon her writing, which is itself a kind of burning: "The typewriter is overheated, my mouth is burning."

What makes Rich's poem so strikingly different from Lowell's "For the Union Dead" is the way it has abandoned itself to the present with rueful determination: "In America we have only the present tense," she writes in her pressured conclusion. In Lowell's poem memory has provided a network of recollections and historical reference whose felt presence makes him powerless before the present-day vulgarity of American life. However baffled Rich's narrator appears, it is clear in her poem that she refuses to be paralyzed by what she has understood.

1

Rich's engagement with the American past has always been different from Lowell's. Rather than providing the material for elegy, it has licensed a fierce optimism. She has for a long time been interested in American life as registered and suffered by those not in power, those not directly responsible for it, and especially women: life in the Massachusetts Bay Colony as experienced by Anne Bradstreet; the Civil War through the eyes of Mary Boykin Chesnut ("Charleston in the Eighteen-Sixties"). Rich has also written about isolated pioneer figures, whose "un-articulate" lives preserved qualities gone underground—qualities which she, in her poetry, would like to make available to the present. Increasingly in the 1970s that interest has taken on a political cast in connection with the women's movement and feminism. Her prose study, *Of Woman Born: Motherhood as Experience and Institution* (1976)—parts autobiography, history, anthropology—is the most ambitious sign of her commitment to expressing and investigating the unexpressed feelings of women. But it is important to remember that this has been a long-standing concern of Rich's poetry. People who frame questions about the effect of her ideological commitment upon her poetry are, I think, looking in the wrong direction. Part of the ideological commitment is *to* poetry and the special powers of its language to probe and reveal. The critic's job is to help judge from poem to poem whether Rich is finding an adequate language for the dramatic situations she discovers and projects, and for the investigative powers she believes poetry to possess.

In the final poem of *Necessities of Life* (1966), "Face to Face," for example, Rich imagines a new condition of speech, modelled on the exchange between two pioneer figures, a husband and wife about to be re-united after a long separation. The poem is breath- · less with tension and with the envy felt by the modern speaker for the frontier's stern, adventurous and isolated life:

> Never to be lonely like that—
> the Early American figure on the beach
> in black coat and knee-breeches
> scanning the didactic storm in privacy,
>
> Never to hear the prairie wolves
> in their lunar hilarity
> circling one's little all, one's claim
> to be Law and Prophets
>
> for all that lawlessness,
> never to whet the appetite
> weeks early, for a face, a hand
> longed-for and dreaded—
>
> How people used to meet!
> starved, intense, the old
> Christmas gifts saved up till spring,
> and the old plain words,
>
> and each with his God-given secret,
> spelled out through months of snow and silence,
> burning under the bleached scalp; behind dry lips
> a loaded gun.

Rich has provided a syntax of infinitives and exclamations, of elided main verbs, for these scenes of stress and expectation, of a loneliness which sharpens the senses. She writes, as Albert Gelpi points out, "a poetry of dialogue and of the furious effort to break through to dialogue."[3] It is the "furious effort" which shows through in "Face to Face." The last line recalls the first line of Emily Dickinson's "My Life had stood—a Loaded Gun," and Rich's poem more than barely resists the radiance which Dickinson experiences once her "Master" appears and her release has come:

> And do I smile, such cordial light
> Upon the Valley glow—
> It is as a Vesuvian face
> Had let its pleasure through—

For Rich the meeting which closes "Face to Face" is as perilous as the solitude and freedom which precede it. The poem captures the absolute dependence of one condition upon the other, the mixed sense of danger and fulfilled desire when the man and woman come together again. "Trying to Talk with a Man" was one of Rich's subjects long before she wrote a poem with that title (1971). But the way she was to imagine such conversations changed over the years. A conversation "From an Old House in America" (1974) is significantly different from the exchange foretold between the two frontier figures of "Face to Face" nine years before. These two meetings bracket an important period of change in Rich's career. In the later, longer poem, toward the close, a man and woman face one another.

> *what will you undertake*
> she said
>
> *will you punish me for history*
> he said
>
> *what will you undertake*
> she said
>
> *do you believe in collective guilt*
> he said
>
> *let me look in your eyes*
> she said

What is missing in a dialogue of this sort is exactly the "furious effort to break through" which characterizes Rich's best work and the parity of partners in "Face to Face." The two figures in "From an Old House . . ." seem locked into position, without the coiled sexual tension of the earlier poem. At the end of "From an Old House . . ." Rich redirects the "loaded gun" of "Face to Face." Once again drawing upon the appeal of an earlier American loneliness, she is speaking this time of women's perilous attempts to find new and individual images for their lives:

> Isolation, the dream
> of the frontier woman
>
> leveling her rifle along
> the homestead fence
>
> still snares our pride
> —a suicidal leaf
>
> laid under the burning-glass
> in the sun's eye
>
> Any woman's death diminishes me

The "loaded gun" here promises only hostility and fear, without the entwined sense of sexual release, of pent-up love, which it carries in "Face to Face." The final line of the poem—"Any woman's death diminishes me"—alludes to Donne's famous line. Its shock value drains away fairly quickly on second reading. Rich knows, of course, that Donne's meditation doesn't refer to the death of men alone, and her own version seems less "true" than simply being a signal, a semaphore, saying that certain kinds of language from the past just won't do. The line is a deliberate narrowing of focus, an unsubtle way of talking about a subject Rich treats with as much point and with more complexity in images which in this same poem precede the "put-down" of Donne. The subject of this poem is women's dream of isolation. The loaded gun is that of the watchful frontier woman at her stockade, and Rich imagines, with a great deal of psychological penetration, that this dream also "snares" a woman's pride. It may be like a "suicidal leaf" (the half-rhyme "life" close to the surface) ready for combustion under the burning-glass.

I have used this example for two reasons. First, to cite one instance of the way Rich's feminism has come forward in her recent writing. Second, and more important, to suggest that the shock value of a line like "Any woman's death diminishes me"—and our agreement or disagreement with its place as *poetry*—should not blind us to the fact that elsewhere in the same work Rich is continuing a task more effective as poetry and more profoundly political. Rich's images—like the "loaded gun" of "Face to Face" and "From an Old House . . ."—often attach themselves in the mind to feelings of ardor and tension. Sometimes, as in "Face to Face," the poem is pitched toward a meeting or a reconciliation. The main action takes place in stillness, an isolated concentration to find the "old plain words," the "God-given secret," which will, in the meetings dreaded and desired, both explode and reach out for understanding. In the later assertiveness of "From an Old House . . ." the "loaded gun" defines boundaries of self, a stockade within which exploration and attention to the self are taking place. No immediate release is promised. But in both these examples, Rich is straining toward a charged language which will make the self, at last, palpable.

Rich undertakes to cross limits which George Eliot, for fiction, had sharply felt and defined:

> If we had a keen vision and feeling of all ordinary human life, it would be like hearing the grass grow and the squirrel's heart beat, and we should die of that roar which lies on the other side of silence.

Rich's poetry by contrast demands that "keen vision" of the inner life and a language which can express it. Her marked preference for the present tense with a floating or broken syntax, her attempts at implied dialogue—the elements of her writing which I have been discussing so far—are at the service of a pointed eloquence. Writing about the self is not self-exposure; it is a model of how we make the self available, visible, accessible to others.

Rich conceives of poems as instruments of exploration and discovery, with images her principal tools, as in "Planetarium":

> I am an instrument in the shape
> of a woman trying to translate pulsations
> into images   for the relief of the body
> and the reconstruction of the mind.

Composing in charged phrases shifts attention to her images, draws the pulse of the poem to them and away from verbs. In many of Rich's poems the images—close to the truth of dreams— rest close to one another in a complexly realized present. This was something she might have learned from Pound through Olson or Williams ("To break the pentameter that was the first heave"). But in a way special to her Rich appropriates the manner to the coil and recoil of emotions. Her ardor transmutes traditional modernist materials. Above all, she puts them at the service of dialogue. What marks her off from poets we have been discussing— Bishop, Lowell, Merrill—is the explicit demand her speakers make not only to understand but *to be understood*. They fight off the notion that insights remain solitary, unshared, dribble off into the past. What's more, her poems, however public in reference, proceed in a tone of intimate argument, as if understanding—political as well as private—is only manifest in the tones with which we explain ourselves to lovers, friends, our closest selves. Whether this radical intensity can be attained and sustained is the question George Eliot asked in *Middlemarch*, and the one Rich asks again and again as her poems make the attempt.

2

In "When We Dead Awaken" Adrienne Rich has written a moving and direct account of her career and the special difficulties of a woman becoming a poet. She speaks of writing for particular

men—her father, teachers—and of taking the definition of her vocation from male masters of the craft—Frost, Dylan Thomas,
Donne, Auden, MacNeice, Stevens, Yeats. The young woman

> goes to poetry or fiction looking for *her* way of being in the
> world, since she too has been putting words and images to-
> gether; she is looking eagerly for guides, maps, possibilities;
> and over and over in the "words' masculine persuasive force"
> of literature she comes up against something that negates
> everything she is about: she meets the image of Woman in
> books written by men.[4]

Still, looking back at her work of that period—the polished stanzas and formal achievements of *A Change of World* and *The Dia-
mond Cutters*—Rich was "startled because beneath the conscious
craft are glimpses of the split I even then experienced between the
girl who wrote poems, who defined herself in writing poems, and
the girl who was to define herself by her relationships with men."
She speaks particularly of the poem "Aunt Jennifer's Tigers" which
she at that time (she was still in college) thought of as portraying
an imaginary woman. But, as Rich was later to remark, Aunt Jennifer "suffers from the opposition of her imagination, [jungle
scenes] worked out in tapestry," and her imprisoning domestic
life. (Uncle's "massive" wedding ring sits heavily upon her finger.)

In long narrative poems like "The Perennial Answer" and "Au-
tumn Equinox" Rich was clearly drawn to try out the voices of the
trapped, lonely, desperate wives who inhabit Frost's dramatic monologues—turning them inside out, as it were. She was also clearly
attracted by the stern, self-determining heroines (and heroes) of
Yeats's lyrics (for example, his "To a Friend Whose Work Has
Come to Nothing"). In her *Selected Poems*, the protagonist of
"Afterward" is identified as a woman, though in the original
youthful version it had been a man. Rich altered the pronouns in
the 1974 version "not simply as a matter of fact but because they
alter, for me, the dimensions of the poem." The change puts the
poem in closer touch with its formidable models, the strong women,
like Lady Gregory, whom Yeats admired. Doing so, it admits a

closer kinship with such characters than the younger poet evidently dared to establish.

> Now that your hopes are shamed, you stand
> At last believing and resigned,
>   . . . .
> We who know limits now give room
> To one who grows to fit her doom.

In Rich's poetry there were explosive materials from the start. "In those years formalism was part of the strategy—like asbestos gloves, it allowed me to handle materials I couldn't pick up barehanded."[5] But formalism wasn't the only protective cover. In "Unsounded," a poem whose imagery of solitary navigators anticipates a little the lonely explorations of "Diving into the Wreck," a lot of the resolute spirit is dispersed by an Arnoldian close, a touch of "To Marguerite." "Each his own Magellan," yes, but "These are latitudes revealed / Separate to each."

Still, in this period of apprenticeship Rich was guided by instinct to the literary modes and postures through which she could express a smouldering and independent nature—one which impressed itself more directly in later work. It is interesting how, in the mannerly tones of her Frostian narratives, she goes intuitively to the core frustration of women dwindling into marriage. She is also not blinded by the glittering surround of heroic figures to whom she is in other ways drawn. In "Euryclea's Tale" (1958), impersonating Ulysses's old nurse, or in "The Knight," playing the critic of heroes herself, she is marvelously penetrating about the burdens and derelictions of traditional warriors. "Who will unhorse this rider / and free him from between / the walls of iron" ("The Knight"). "I have to weep when I see it, the grown boy fretting / for a father dawdling among the isles" ("Euryclea's Tale").

Yet still we see the knight "under his crackling banner / he rides like a ship in sail." And Euryclea, baffled and resentful on the part of the boy Telemachus, still can think of Ulysses's vagrancy in more romantic terms:

> But all the time and everywhere
> lies in ambush for the distracted eyeball
> light: light on the ship wracked up in port,
> the chimney-stones, the scar whiter than smoke,
> than her flanks, her hair, that true but aging bride.

The ambush here is the storyteller's own susceptibility to all fac-
ets of the story, to the all-encompassing light in which Ulysses's
travels may be viewed ("the driftwood stranger and the rooted
boy / whose eyes will have nothing then to ask the sea"—i.e., when
his father has returned).

Wandering in the blazing sunlight of "Villa Adriana," the young
poet's temptation had been to reconstruct in dream the emperor
Hadrian's hubris, "the columned roofs under the blazing sky, /
The courts so open." One book later in "Antinoüs: the Diaries"
she let the young man, Hadrian's favorite, speak for her attractions
and discontents with the imaginative world she inhabited:

> Then at some house the rumor of truth and beauty
> saturates a room like lilac-water
> in the steam of a bath, fires snap, heads are high,
> gold hair at napes of necks, gold in glasses,
> gold in the throat, poetry of furs and manners.

Antinoüs is filled with nausea, participating in "the old, needless
story,"

> If what I spew on the tiles at last,
> helpless, disgraced, alone,
> is in part what I've swallowed from glasses, eyes,
> motions of hands, opening and closing mouths,
> isn't it also dead gobbets of myself,
> abortive, murdered, or never willed?

In taking on earlier literary modes and historical figures, Rich
very often found an angle of the subject which allowed her to enter the scene guardedly. By the time she wrote "Antinoüs: the Diaries" it was with a measure of self-disgust. Only later, when they
were no longer part of the inherited "poetry of furs and man-

ners"—and through the strange economy of a poet's memory—
was she to welcome back those glints of richness as signs, not of a
transmitted love of surfaces, but as answering to the hidden resources of the spirit. Modulated, in a different key, a chastened
opulence was to be one way of talking about the sunken treasure
of personality—the lost, the suppressed, the unspoken—in Rich's
more disciplined, radical poems. For example, in "Diving into the
Wreck" (1972), one way of talking about confusions of history
and sexuality, the damages, the riches rotting and waiting to be
unlocked, was to imagine them among shifting underwater forms,
"the silver, copper, vermeil cargo," the sea-creatures "swaying their
crenellated fans," "the ribs of the disaster / curving their asser-
tion / among the tentative haunters."

But when she published *Snapshots of a Daughter-in-Law* (1963),
Rich was using her "literary" skills ("The Knight," "Euryclea's
Tale" and "Antinoüs: the Diaries" were all collected in this volume) in an irritated way. She had found her subject: fighting free
of what sheltered her, others' homes, others' books and language;
but she had not found her own way of speaking. In the forthright
title poem, the "snapshots of a daughter-in-law" are part of a
highly literary strategy, ironically like "The Wasteland," testing
traditional poetic representations of women against deflating modern instances of women's daily experiences, inner strengths and
resentments:

> When to her lute Corinna sings
> neither words nor music are her own
>
>   . . . .
> Sigh no more, ladies.
>   Time is male
> and in his cups drinks to the fair.
> Bemused by gallantry, we hear
> our mediocrities over-praised,
> indolence read as abnegation.

The literary irritation is twinned with a mounting bitterness far
more central, the discovery of "the silent isolation of minds in

marriage," as Helen Vendler puts it.[6] Rich's own way of talking about the late 1950s and early 1960s is important.

> I was writing very little, partly from fatigue, that female fa-
> tigue of suppressed anger and the loss of contact with her
> own being; partly from the discontinuity of female life with
> its attention to small chores, errands, work that others con-
> stantly undo, small children's constant needs. . . . Trying to
> look back and understand that time I have tried to analyze
> the real nature of the conflict. Most, if not all, human lives
> are full of fantasy—passive day-dreaming which need not be
> acted on. But to write poetry or fiction, or even to think
> well, is not to fantasize, or to put fantasies on paper. For a
> poem to coalesce, for a character or an action to take shape,
> there has to be an imaginative transformation of reality
> which is in no way passive. And a certain freedom of the
> mind is needed—freedom to press on, to enter the currents of
> your thought like a glider pilot . . . to question, to chal-
> lenge, to conceive of alternatives, perhaps to the very life you
> are living at that moment. . . . Now, to be maternally with
> small children all day in the old way, to be with a man in the
> old way of marriage, requires a holding-back, a putting-aside
> of that imaginative activity, and seems to demand instead a
> kind of conservatism. I want to make it clear that I am *not*
> saying that in order to write well, or think well, it is necessary
> to become unavailable to others, or to become a devouring
> ego. . . . But to be a female human being trying to fulfill
> traditional female functions in a traditional way *is* in direct
> conflict with the subversive function of the imagination. The
> word traditional is important here. There must be ways, and
> we will be finding out more and more about them, in which
> the energy of creation and the energy of relation can be
> united. But in those earlier years, I always felt the conflict as
> a failure of love in myself.[7]

Distinctions fall away—Yeats's dictum that the poet must choose between perfection of the life and perfection of the work, for ex-ample. The pain and conflict which Rich records in her account would energize her work for years to come—still does, even after the death of her husband and the growth of her children, no longer at home, into young adulthood. How these conflicts were worked out in her poetry was to be the story especially of *Snapshots of a Daughter-in-Law* and the three books which followed it, *Necessities of Life* (1966), *Leaflets* (1969) and *The Will to Change* (1971). These were restless and intense, an uncertain threading through difficult areas of personality and language. With *Snapshots*, Rich began dating each of her poems by year, a way of limiting their claims, of signalling that they spoke only for their moment. The poems were seen as instruments of passage, of self-scrutiny and resolve in the present.

3

The young woman of "Snapshots of a Daughter-in-Law" had asked: "has Nature shown / her household books to you, daughter-in-law, / that her sons never saw?" Even if the answer to that question were yes, converting Nature's accounts into verse was another matter. Rich's discomfort with the problem shows up in a number of poems about marriage in which a wife addresses her husband. In the key poem, "A Marriage in the 'Sixties," she describes that state of being together in which

> Two strangers, thrust for life upon a rock,
> may have at last the perfect hour of talk
> that language aches for; still—
> two minds, two messages.

The ache is apparent, the gestures of dialogue falling away into a line asserting separate selves. In this poem Rich resolves the division partially by re-imagining the divided figures as astral twins:

> Dear fellow-particle, electric dust
> I'm blown with—ancestor
> to what euphoric cluster—
> see how particularity dissolves
> in all that hints of chaos. Let one finger
> hover toward you from There
> and see this furious grain

> suspend its dance to hang
> beside you like your twin.

The solution here is a kind of cosmic dissolution, the partners joined by tender address and suspended, dwarfed by galaxies. This was a tone Lowell would adopt at much the same time, in "The Flaw":

> Hope of the hopeless launched and cast adrift
> on the great flaw that gives the final gift.
>
> Dear Figure curving like a questionmark,
> how will you hear my answer in the dark?

Or again, in "Night Sweat": "absolve me, help me, Dear Heart, as you bear / this world's dead weight and cycle on your back."

But Rich's momentary resting with tender address, figures joined in frail decay, was not one she would sustain. There was another sense of Nature the galaxies had come to signify—one of blazing independence and will. "Is it that in starry places / We see the things we long to see / In fiery iconography?" Rich asked that question as early as "For the Conjuction of Two Planets" in her first book. "Novella," another poem on marriage in *Snapshots*, gives bare stage directions for a quarrelling couple: "Two people in a room, speaking harshly. / One gets up, goes out to walk." What brings it to a close? "The door closes behind him. / Outside, separate as minds, / the stars too come alight." No disintegration here; instead, a defiant comfort in the redoubtable stars which come out "separate as minds."

Rich returns to that "old transfusion" in "Orion" (1965). The constellation, welcomed as a fierce ally, half-brother, offers an alternative to the stiflement of home:

> Indoors I bruise and blunder,
> break faith, leave ill enough
> alone . . .
>   . . . .
> A man reaches behind my eyes
> and finds them empty

> a woman's head turns away
> from my head in the mirror
> children are dying my death
> and eating crumbs of my life.

There were to be in Rich's poems of the 1960s a number of these images of exposure and isolated strength, sometimes, as in "Orion," felt as guilt ("when I look you back / it's with a starlike eye / shooting its cold and egotistical spear"). At other times she comes on these images with relief at having broken the old vicarious shelters, as in "The Roofwalker." Rich adopts with fierce determination a figure inspired by Simone de Beauvoir for the new woman "more merciless to herself than history," appearing like a helicopter in "Snapshots of a Daughter-in-Law":

> her fine blades making the air wince

> but her cargo
> no promise then:
> delivered
> palpable
> ours.

This was a prophetic image, but one even more valuable for Rich when she came to use it in a less prophetic way in her next book, *Necessities of Life*. In "In the Woods" she appropriates the image for her *own* pleasurable freedom:

> My soul, my helicopter, whirred
> distantly, by habit, over
> the old pond with the half-drowned boat
>
> toward which it always veers
> for consolation: ego's Arcady:
> leaving the body stuck
> like a leaf against a screen.
>
> Happiness! how many times
> I've stranded on that word,
> at the edge of that pond; seen
> as if through tears, the dragon-fly—

> only to find it all
> going differently for once
> this time: my soul wheeled back
> and burst into my body.
>
> Found! Ready or not.
> If I move now, the sun
> naked between the trees
> will melt me as I lie.

In a moment of play, both childlike and sensuous, Rich relaxes with the self-assertiveness she found hard to handle in her previous book. *Necessities of Life* is a remarkable collection. In its mainly pastoral setting, the New England woods, Rich plays out, with freedom and feeling, a number of contradictory roles, which in the urban domesticity of *Snapshots* and in her later books had and would conflict with one another. In *Necessities of Life* she seems to enjoy a precarious immunity, the chance to experience a various self. "To have it out at last / on your own premises," she says of Emily Dickinson. The title poem acts out, metaphorically, with wry satisfaction, the rebirth of a tough little self:

> wolfed almost to shreds,
> I learned to make myself
>
> unappetizing. Scaly as a dry bulb
> thrown into a cellar
>
> I used myself, let nothing use me.
>   . . . .
>   Soon
> practice may make me middling perfect, I'll
>
> dare inhabit the world
> trenchant in motion as an eel, solid
>
> as a cabbage-head. I have invitations:
> a curl of mist steams upward
>
> from a field, visible as my breath,
> houses along a road stand waiting

like old women knitting, breathless
to tell their tales.

What is odd about *Necessities of Life* is the way the book moves
from an emerging self to poems where Rich does, repeatedly, a
vanishing act. The very sun that frees and fires her "In the Woods"
blanches her into a "cradle-tomb" in the next poem, "The Corpse-
Plant." Back indoors she stares at a cluster of corpse-plants (children call them Indian pipes):

Only death's insect whiteness
crooks its neck in a tumbler
where I placed its sign by choice.

In the love poems as well she ponders her disappearance:

We're slowly bleaching

with the days, the hours, and the years.
We are getting finer than ever,

time is wearing us to silk,
to sheer spiderweb.
                                    ("Side by Side")

I am gliding backward away from those who knew me
as the moon grows thinner and finally shuts its lantern.
I can be replaced a thousand times,
a box containing death.
When you put out your hand to touch me
you are already reaching toward an empty space.
                                    ("Moth Hour")

The marriage poems are poems of attrition, prompting Rich to
images like the one that closes "The Parting: I": "Every knot is a
knife / where two strands tangle to rust." Or, describing "The
Knot" of blood at the heart of the Queen Anne's lace: "the tiny
dark-red spider / sitting in the whiteness of the bridal web." Often
in this volume frustrations are resolved by focusing on images of
natural danger or decay, or by withdrawal. In "Mourning Picture"
the scene recalls a painting by Edwin Romanzo Elmer, a memorial

to his daughter Effie. The parents are seated on a lawn in mourning for the young girl whose doll is still in its wicker pram "gazing
at western Massachusetts." Rich has chosen to tell the poem spec-
trally through the eyes of the young dead daughter. Or again, writing of her own grandmother, Rich says, of herself, "A young girl,
thought sleeping, is certified dead." The poem is called "Halfway."

> In the field the air writhes, a heat-pocket.
> Masses of birds revolve, blades
> of a harvester.
> The sky is getting milkily white,
> a sac of light is ready to burst open.
>
> Time of hailstones and rainbow.
> My life flows North. At last I understand.
> A young girl, thought sleeping, is certified dead.
> A tray of expensive waxen fruit,
> she lies arranged on the spare-room coverlid.
>
> To sit by the fire is to become another woman,
> red hair charring to grey,
> green eyes grappling with the printed page,
> voice flailing, flailing the uncomprehending.
> My days lie open, listening, grandmother.

Written when Rich was thirty-five, Dante's halfway point
through the journey of life, the poem is "halfway" in another
sense. It mediates between the ways Rich has of imagining herself
in this book: the selves bleaching into death and the breathless
tone of the more assertive self Rich musters often when she is
alone in her poems. Masked in the revolving birds' "blades / of a
harvester" is the helicopter ego from "In the Woods." Rich very
often gains strength from poems about women in her family; her
frequent poems to and about her sister are loving and take pleasure
in their relaxed sympathy for one another. "Halfway," in touch
with her grandmother, almost seems to revive the young granddaughter, imagined prematurely dead. Her days are magically
transformed to a listening book. The tone of the ending picks up

the charged anticipation at the end of the opening poem, "Necessities of Life," where "houses along a road stand waiting / like old women knitting, breathless / to tell their tales." The young woman, ready in these poems to listen to the old wives' tales, is clearly eager and gathering strength to tell her own.

It is strange then that the assertive self of some of these poems does not penetrate the poems of love and marriage; that those poems are lyrics of disintegration and the fine winnowing of self. *Necessities of Life* is in a delicate equilibrium, fully open to those rich and contradictory feelings. What is more astonishing is that it closes with a poem which breaks that pattern. The poem—we have looked at it already—is "Face to Face" and in it, almost for the first time, Rich anticipates bringing together both the energies of the solitary ego and the energies of dialogue, of a lovers' relationship. The poem hopes for the nourishment of a marriage through the charged revelation of the inner life:

> and each with his God-given secret,
> spelled out through months of snow and silence,
> burning under the bleached scalp; behind dry lips
> a loaded gun.

What language they were to speak was yet to be discovered.

4

The books which follow *Necessities of Life* seem driven by the craving for new ways of talking, so that the asserted, palpable self might be accepted as the basis of relation between lovers, husband and wife, friends. "I wanted to choose words that even you / would have to be changed by" ("Implosions"). Gone the old instinct that the ego must dwindle in relationships. Her poems lie like wishes on the pages. They make the further implicit claim— with an ardor worthy of *Middlemarch*—that the recharged and regenerated selves are the only true basis of political change. Both her radicalism of the late 1960s and her feminism in the 1970s, at their most convincing, rest on self-scrutiny and individual growth.

Leaflets, The Will to Change and *Diving into the Wreck* ask to be
read less like books of detachable polished poems and more like
journals—patient, laconic, eloquent but dating themselves, provisional instruments of passage in the present. One doesn't turn
back. (They are, for example, not the kind of journals into which
one hundred new poems could be dropped retrospectively, as was
the case in the second edition of Robert Lowell's *Notebook*.)

It is striking how many of these poems are about fresh starts, as
if that position had to be re-imagined constantly to keep up the intensity of the verse, bypass disappointments, overcome the pain of
broken connections. Here are some examples from poems written
throughout the period 1968-74:

>   . . . I am thinking how we can use what we have
>   to invent what we need.
>   ("Leaflets," 1968)

> How you broke open, what sheathed you
> until this moment
> I know nothing about it
> my ignorance of you amazes me
> now that I watch you
> starting to give yourself away
> to the wind
>   ("November 1968")

> To pull yourself up by your own roots; to eat the last meal in
> your old neighborhood.
>   ("Shooting Script," 1970)

> *The Fact of a Doorframe*
> means there is something to hold
> onto with both hands
> while slowly thrusting my forehead against the wood
>   . . . .
> Now, again, poetry,
> violent, arcane, common,
> hewn of the commonest living substance
> into archway, portal, frame

> I grasp for you, your bloodstained splinters, your
> ancient and stubborn poise
> > ("The Fact of a Doorframe," 1974)

The threshold is an apt metaphor for Rich's recent poems which are, by their nature, more about method, about preparing oneself, about "the will to change," than they are visions of a final resting place. Now, explorers and scientists and field-workers make frequent appearances, the envied projection of a self out to dig away or escape historical conditioning. She writes of Caroline Herschel, the astronomer, discovering new stars in the eighteenth century; or Dr. Itard making his painstaking observations of the wild child raised among wolves; or of the woman anthropologist in Africa "completely protected on all sides / by volcanoes"

> In her dreams, her notebooks, still
> private as maiden diaries,
> the mountain gorillas move through their life term;
> their gentleness survives
> observation

The poet envies

> the pale gorilla-scented dawn
> she wakes into, the stream where she washes her hair
> the camera-flash of her quiet
> eye.
> > ("The Observer," 1968)

Much is brought forward here: the withdrawal into dreams and isolation as a way of short-circuiting history; dreams as notebooks and maiden diaries; the immunity of the dreamer (her observations don't threaten the primitive life around her, whereas Dr. Itard's study of the wild wolf-child *does* threaten the child's natural purity).

The problem for Rich's explorers is suggested by the final metaphor of "The Observer": "the camera-flash of her quiet / eye." What the anthropologist learns about primitive responses is hers in privileged silence. The isolation—punning—of the single word *eye* at the end of the poem signals a momentary accord of vision and ego. But Rich was to use the metaphor of photos and film in more complicated situations and in circumstances when the speaker was not alone. *The Will to Change* is filled with such poems. In "The Photograph of the Unmade Bed" the separate hearts and minds of the lovers are explained in terms of the gap between permanently recorded act and the intention or will behind it, or between photograph and poem.

> Cruelty is rarely conscious
> One slip of the tongue
>
> one exposure
> among so many

The pun of "exposure" cruelly shows up the difference between the cold recorded image and the human vulnerabilities that cause a rift and misunderstanding.

> In a flash I understand
> how poems are unlike photographs
>
> (the one saying   *This could be*
> the other   *This was*
>
> The image
> isn't responsible
>
> for our uses of it
> It is intentionless

The poem itself is a moving attempt to heal a breach, to animate the blunt record of a convulsive separation. It is set out in four units, printed in alternate quadrants of two pages, like four photos pasted in diagonal pairs in an album. The effect for the reader, going from one juxtaposed poem to another, is almost like an attempt to connect four close "takes," as Rich moves from one shot, one version of her feelings, to another. She implies that the purpose of a poem is to penetrate tangled feelings as the mere surface record of a harsh deed or word will not. In the final stanza she faces the difficulties and implications of failure and, in the final image, tries to bring motion out of silence, to translate isolated images into a clarifying gesture of reconciliation. But it is hard to tell whether the lips at the end are those of the dying or the reviving self:

> This crust of bread we try to share
> this name traced on a window
>
> this word I paste together
> like a child fumbling
>
> with paste and scissors
> this writing in the sky with smoke
>
> this silence
>
> this lettering chalked on the ruins
> this alphabet of the dumb
>
> this feather held to lips
> that still breathe and are warm

The gap between the candid eye of "The Observer" and the figure trying to transmit her images to save a marriage in "The Photograph of the Unmade Bed" is perhaps unbridgeable. But Rich has always felt the challenge of trying to make the feelings available in images and metaphors. The forms she has attempted in her poems answer to a feeling of urgency. Like "The Photograph of the Unmade Bed," "Pierrot le Fou" displays a fevered interest in film as an instrument of reconciliation. The poem will capture some of the fluidity of film, as she puts it in "Images for Godard":

> the mind of the poet is the only poem
> the poet is at the movies
>
> dreaming the film-maker's dream but differently
> free in the dark as if asleep

> free in the dusty beams of the projector
> the mind of the poet is changing
>
> the moment of change is the only poem

For the poet "dreaming the film-maker's dream," image and action are one. Once again the image is the inevitable charged particle for Rich, a way to make visible gestures more responsive to inner contradictions and change.

Rich had, in *Leaflets*, begun to write *ghazals*, a form borrowed from the Urdu poet Ghalib, and anticipating the fluid play of images she described in "Images for Godard." The *ghazal* had a minimum of five couplets, each free-standing and independent of the others. "The continuity and unity flow from the associations and images playing back and forth among the couplets in any single *ghazal*."[8] Each of her *ghazals* was dated, as were the letters, "pieces" and finally "films" and "photographs" which make up *The Will to Change*. To cut images as free as possible from ordinary temporal sequence became Rich's aim, convinced as she was that "In America we have only the present tense." Syntactical irregularities became a means of self-interrogation, as in this scene in an old house:

> To float like a dead man in a sea of dreams
> and half those dreams being dreamed by someone else.
>
> Fifteen years of sleepwalking with you,
> wading against the tide, and with the tide.
>   ("The Blue Ghazals")

These sentence fragments raise ghosts of questions and conclusions. Being incomplete, they expose fears and loyalties at the same moment, and their grammar suggests how such emotions float entwined and unresolved in the mind.

The "Shooting Script" which makes up the final section of *The Will to Change* extends Rich's attempt at finding a notation true to the movement of the feelings. Its fourteen poems cover eight months of her life, from November 1969 to July 1970. These are spare instructions for a photographer of the inner self. A shooting script in another sense, it is a way of gunning out, of performing yet again the ceremony of breaking free. Open to contradictions, conducted in terse cuts from one set of images to another, "Shooting Script" begins with an attempt at dialogue and ends with the poet alone, pulling herself loose, eating the last meal in her old neighborhood. At the outset of the poem she tries for these exchanges, described elsewhere ("Our Whole Life") as "Words bitten thru words / meanings burnt-off like paint / under the blowtorch." The pain and failure of communication in the opening sections is expressed as much by the silences between terse one-line units as by the struggle for adequate images to *describe* a dialogue:

> We were bound on the wheel of an endless conversation.
>
> Inside this shell, a tide waiting for someone to enter.
>
> A monologue waiting for you to interrupt it.

Evoking an unending cycle of harmonies and violence—and placed in the past tense—this section tells largely a tale of failure, the failure of the method Rich has often used in which images are trusted to make her subjective self available to the person she loves. Part One of the two main parts of "Shooting Script" ends with the lovers confronting each another:

> Someone who never said, "What do you feel?" someone who sat across from me, taking the crumbs of wax as I picked them apart and handed them over.

"Shooting Script" marks a turning point in Rich's poetry. The sequence had aimed to open, guard and translate the most individual feelings. It represents the extreme of Rich's technical experiments; *The Will to Change* is filled with *ghazals*, fluid syntax imitating the methods of film, "letters," "pieces," "photographs"— beating on every possible door, for more and more provisional devices to release the self and make it palpable. The frustrations of "Shooting Script"—the failed relationship of its opening sections—

lead to a remarkable shift of emphasis in the sequence. Rich turns
away from what she calls "the temptations of the projector" with
its images of pain from the past, its record of individual misunderstandings. She begins to look to the historical misunderstandings
behind battered sexual relationships, the long record of conflicts
between men and women.

In one section of "Shooting Script" Rich imagines herself an anthropologist collating the shards which will recall the dialect of
those for whom "the sole of the foot is a map, the palm of the
hand a letter, / learned by heart and worn close to the body." Her
more subjective aims in poetry now shade into the desire to inves-
tigate and gain access to our most unconditioned experiences. Late
in the poem she imagines safeguarding a young niece from the in-
cursions of education and history:

> They come to you with their descriptions of your soul.
>   . . . .
> They believe your future has a history and that
> it is themselves.
>   . . . .
> You hang among them like the icon in a Russian
> play; living your own intenser life behind
> the lamp they light in front of you.
>   . . . .
> You are a mirror lost in a brook, an eye reflecting
> a torrent of reflections.
>
> You are a letter written, folded, burnt to ash,
> and mailed in an envelope to another continent.

This is Rich at her most eloquent. For one thing, writing for
women in her family—her mother, her sister—always calls forth a
special intensity in her work. For another thing, she rises to the
challenge of encouraging a young woman to be free of the definitions of self which family and history place upon her. It is entirely
characteristic of Rich, in a poem which begins in failure, not to accept the sexual failure and the failure of communication as tragic
circumstances of life. "Shooting Script" instead looks to find new

ways to explain the irritations, anger and humiliations with which
it begins. By the end the speaker, both in the poem to her niece
and in her own resolve, is prepared to make, yet again, another
fresh start.

5

The new investigations are those promised in the poem "Diving
into the Wreck," adventures behind the common definitions of
sexuality and beyond the damages done by acculturation and conditioning. It is here also that Rich makes her strongest political
identification with feminism, in her attempts to define experiences
unique to women or to define the damages done by false definitions of sexual identity. Into her images she has been able to concentrate much of what has always been in her poetry: what it is
like to feel oppressed, betrayed and unfulfilled. The explicit identification with feminism sometimes sets poems off balance. But this
is a matter of presentation and not—as some critics have suggested—because Rich has radically changed the direction or in-
terests of her writing. "Translations" is a good example. Reading
in translation the poems of a young woman, she senses a tempera-
mental kinship:

>   she's a woman of my time
>
>   obsessed
>
>   with Love, our subject:
>   we've trained it like ivy to our walls
>   baked it like bread in our ovens
>   worn it like lead on our ankles
>   watched it through binoculars as if
>   it were a helicopter
>   bringing food to our famine
>   or the satellite
>   of a hostile power

The movement of Rich's verse captures not only the nourishing
power of the woman poet's careful genius for love but also its

power to entrap her. The stressed verbs propel four successive lines, so that it is hard, against that urgent rhythm, to separate the nurturing from the corrosive, the domestic from the imprisoning (an interior rhyme of *bread* and *lead*). The familiar image of helicopter returns, this time to suggest love as a dangerous projection of the ego.

The poem goes on to imagine the foreign poet's daily life. She tries to make a call from a phone booth. It rings unanswered in a man's bedroom. "She hears him telling someone else / *Never mind. She'll get tired.*" She also hears him telling her story to her "sister"

> who becomes her enemy
> and will in her own time
> light her own way to sorrow
>
> ignorant of the fact this way of grief
> is shared, unnecessary
> and political

I have always felt that too much is underlined in these last two lines; that a neatening false to the complexity of the poem has taken place. Saying that the grief is "unnecessary and political" seems a dubious summary, suggesting in a beguiling way that betrayal is eradicable in a sexual revolution, though the poem itself suggests how love and betrayal are bound to men and women both. "This way of grief," it seems to me, would be more fully shared without the final two adjectives.

Yet these are problems growing out of the tireless demand Rich's poetry has always made for reconciliation, for individual and social change. Her mining for images is designed to produce what George Eliot called the "keen vision and feeling of all ordinary human life." Rich's poems are bound to be restless, bound to be looking constantly for new beginnings, because they will never resign themselves to solitude.

The pressure under which she writes has led her in new directions. Her prose study *Of Woman Born* represents several years of study and finally brings together materials from anthropology, history and from her own life as both child and mother. "But I did not choose this subject; it had long ago chosen me," Rich says in the preface. It does indeed grow out of the tensions between the sexes which her poems have always explored, asking this time—and appropriately in prose—whether they are ingrained in the biological differences between men and women or historically conditioned. The central effort of feminism, but here explored through the special experience of motherhood, the way she has felt it and the way it has been defined in Western societies. Her argument is too complicated to summarize. For this essay on her verse, its importance lies first and foremost in the fact that she has been impelled to make such an argument—that, after two decades of writing poetry, exploring the tangled balances of power between individuals, she is now looking outside those particular experiences to the larger conditioning—historical, racial—brought to bear on every relationship, to the "mothering" each individual has had, and to the woman's special experience in becoming the mother of others.

> In my twenties, I gave birth to three children within four years: a radicalizing experience. As a mother, I experienced great internal violence; yet it was as a mother that I first became politicized. . . . I wrote [this book] in part for the young woman I once was, divided between body and mind, wanting to give her the book she was seeking, a perspective which would clarify the past and open ways of thinking and changing in the future.[9]

What effect this book will have on Rich's future writing is hard to tell. But it is clear that Rich's sustained prose effort and large historical framework will take some of the pressure off what she expects of individual poems. Especially in the early 1970s, one could hear in Rich's poems the growing frustrations and anger accumulated by re-imagining again and again the fresh starts, the efforts at reconciliation. Titles like "Burning Oneself In" and "Burning Oneself Out" speak for themselves. "The Phenomenology of Anger" (1972) acts out some of women's deepest night-

mares and cravings for violence, but it also speaks Rich's special
frustration as an image-maker, all those years hoping for dialogue:

> When I dream of meeting
> the enemy, this is my dream:
>
> white acetylene
> ripples from my body
> effortlessly released
> perfectly trained
> on the true enemy
>
> raking his body down to the thread
> of existence
> burning away his lie
> leaving him in a new
> world; a changed
> man

Even redirecting her violence, there is—as those last lines and their
emphatic separation suggest—at the back of Rich's mind a suppressed dream of dialogue and regenerated selves.

And twinned with the anger in these recent poems, there is also
an enlarged awareness—a new voice, I think, in Rich's work—of
the tragedy wrought into human relationships and into the attempts at dialogue and exchange. There are two particularly important examples: on the level of social injustice, her "Meditations
for a Savage Child" and, less general, a poem of blunted love,
"Cartographies of Silence." "Meditations for a Savage Child" is
a remarkable poem based on the documents Truffaut also used so
movingly in his film *L'Enfant Sauvage*, the records of the French
doctor, J. M. Itard (now published as *The Wild Boy of Aveyron*).
Itard had observed and partly "civilized" a savage child in the late
eighteenth century. Rich, perhaps following Truffaut, introduces
excerpts from the doctor's accounts as points of departure for each
of the five sections of her poem. Unlike Truffaut, who chose to
play the part of Itard in his film, Rich often takes on the role of
the child, or ponders what he has to teach her, as she engages in a

series of meditative exchanges with the voice of Itard. The poem is partly a long historical register of Rich's own divided spirit. Itard is an adversary but not an enemy, as they gaze across the ambitious ruins of Enlightenment philosophy. In the solicitous elegance of his prose, she finds words which have been emptied of their meaning: humanity, administrators, protection of the government—the roots of much which would have once engaged her own ardor. But in the mysteries of childrearing, of miseducation, she locates everything which defeats that ardor.

As Helen Vendler points out, the real scarring in this poem rests with parents, the original governors

> they tried to care for you
> tried to teach you to care
> for objects of their caring

"The seductive interchange by which parents barter 'care for you' in exchange for your 'caring' for 'objects of their caring' is glossed by Rich's pun."[10] Speaking to the child in this opening section, Rich is careful to let different vocabularies speak for themselves. We hear Itard in the analytic tones of the moral scientist: "There was a profound indifference to the objects of our pleasures and of our fictitious needs." Then we hear Rich's own solicitude for the child's lack of interest in civilized objects; and then suddenly the direct appeal of the objects themselves:

> to teach you names
> for things
> you did not need

> muslin shirred against the sun
> linen on a sack of feathers
> locks, keys
> boxes with coins inside

The typographical divisions which persist through this section allow us to enter each attitude, each argument, as into a space. The fact that the child does not "need" certain objects is set against the freshness with which they are encountered in the next block of

type, savored like the "muslin shirred against the sun," or reduced
to their elements like the pillow which becomes "linen on a sack
of feathers."

The whole poem allows such counter-impressions while fervently
pursuing the lessons the wild child has to teach us—his scars, for
example. Itard claims that they "bear witness . . . against the
feebleness and insufficiency of man when left entirely to himself,
and in favor of the resources of nature which . . . work openly
to repair and conserve that which she tends secretly to impair and
destroy." Rich, exploring that argument, enters

> A cave of scars!
> ancient, archaic wallpaper
> built up, layer on layer
> from the earliest, dream-white
> to yesterday's, a red-black scrawl
> a red mouth slowly closing
>
> Go back so far there is another language
> go back far enough the language
> is no longer personal
>
> these scars bear witness
> but whether to repair
> or to destruction
> I no longer know

Rich's technique of exploring by images here carries us to the kind
of frontier she wants her poetry to touch. In the poem Itard claims
that the scar on the wild boy's neck is reassuring, removes any
doubts about "the soundness of the underlying parts." Rich has a
more complex response; she identifies with the buried pain.
"When I try to speak / my throat is cut." She comes to imagine
poetry itself—and human speech—as built on scar tissue.

> Yet always the tissue
> grows over, white as silk
>
> hardly a blemish
> maybe a hieroglyph for scream

> Child, no wonder you never wholly
> trusted your keepers

The lines are poised between an almost erotic attraction to the scar and an attempt to alert us to the violence behind it, a brutality and exercise of power which precede human language. This represents, I think, a deeper understanding than the references to the "oppressor's language" in "The Burning of Paper Instead of Children." Equally pained, but with more awareness of the degree to which the screams of human need and pain may or may not be expressed by language and understood.

In "Cartographies of Silence" Rich seems to take up the same problem as it once again affects the private life. Contemplating a break with a lover, she looks at the division she discovers over and over in her poems—the difference between poem and understood dialogue, between individual feeling and a fulfilled relationship.

> A conversation begins with a lie. And each
>
> speaker of the so-called common language feels
> the ice-floe split, the drift apart
>
> as if powerless, as if up against
> a force of nature.

By contrast, "A poem can begin / with a lie. And be torn up." Conversation, she admits, "Inscribes with its unreturning stylus / the isolation it denies." Instead of "the furious effort to break through to dialogue" of her earlier love poems, Rich seems to accept the ingrained limits of her language, or, rather, to have modulated her expectations into a lower key. She seems more at home in the privacy of her poem, and less frustrated by the prospect of silence registered at the end of "Face to Face" ("behind dry lips / a loaded gun"). In "Cartographies of Silence" she speaks in language which yearns for contact at the same time as it takes account of the dangers of those yearnings:

> The silence that strips bare:
> in Dreyer's *Passion of Joan*

Falconetti's face, hair shorn, a great geography
mutely surveyed by the camera

if there were a poetry where this could happen
not as blank spaces or as words

stretched like a skin over meanings
but as silence falls at the end

of a night through which two people
have talked till dawn

In its very title "Cartographies of Silence" sends us back to the
ardor for a knowledge of human relationships which has animated
much of Rich's work. But the poem itself turns an appraising, sad
eye on the large energies involved in a career so fervently directed
outward. It is hard to know, now that some of Rich's force and
passionate intelligence has been directed into prose, just what role
poetry will come to play in her life and in her writing. Critics have
in the past pointed out how much, in her commitment to the notation of present feelings, the pain of the moment, Rich has given
up the traditional retrospective and shaping functions of verse.
Poems like "Meditations for a Savage Child" and "Cartographies
of Silence" show that whatever she has relinquished she has given
up purposefully, that she understands the price of her ardor without giving up her rights to it.

V JOHN ASHBERY
Self-Portrait in a Convex Mirror

In 1972 John Ashbery was invited to read at Shiraz, in Iran, where for several years the Empress had sponsored a festival of music, art, and drama which was remarkable, even notorious, for its modernity: Peter Brook's *Orghast*, Robert Wilson's week-long production *Ka Mountain and GUARDenia Terrace*, Merce Cunningham's dances, the music of Stockhausen and John Cage. Ashbery and another visitor, David Kermani, reported that "to a country without significant modern traditions, still under the spell of its own great past, where a production of Shaw or Ibsen would count as a novelty, such an effort even might seem quixotic." Taking into consideration Iranian critics who demanded Shakespeare first or Chekhov first, Ashbery's own response was delighted and characteristic: "The important thing is to start from the beginning, that is, the present. Oscar Wilde's 'Take care of the luxuries and the necessities will take care of themselves' might well have been the motto of the festival, and its justification."[1] That oversimplifies his view of tradition and modernism, this poet who has rich and felt connections, for example, to Traherne and Marvell as well as to recent poets like Wallace Stevens and Auden and Marianne Moore. But the present is always Ashbery's point of departure: "Before I read modern poetry, the poetry of the past was of really no help to me."[2]

Familiar notions about a poet's development won't quite apply to Ashbery's work. He doesn't return to objects, figures and key incidents which, as the career unfolds, gather increasing symbolic resonance. Nor do his poems refer to one another in any obvious way. Ashbery writes autobiography only inasmuch as he writes about the widening sense of what it is like to gain—or to try to gain—access to his experience. The present is the poem. "I think that any one of my poems might be considered to be a snapshot of whatever is going on in my mind at the time—first of all the desire to write a poem, after that wondering if I've left the oven on or thinking about where I must be in the next hour."[3] Or, more tellingly, in verse ("And *Ut Pictura Poesis* Is Her Name," from *Houseboat Days*):

> The extreme austerity of an almost empty mind
> Colliding with the lush, Rousseau-like foliage of its desire to
>   communicate
> Something between breaths, if only for the sake
> Of others and their desire to understand you and desert you
> For other centers of communication, so that understanding
> May begin, and in doing so be undone.

Like Penelope's web, the doing and undoing of Ashbery's poems is often their subject: fresh starts, repeated collisions of plain talk with the tantalizing and frustrating promises of "poetry." The "desire to communicate" erodes, over a pointed line-break, into hasty beleaguered utterance. Nor does an accumulating personal history provide a frame for him with outlines guiding and determining the future: "Seen from inside all is / Abruptness."

> And the great flower of what we have been twists
> On its stem of earth, for not being
> What we are to become, fated to live in
> Intimidated solitude and isolation.
>
> ("Fragment")

In his images of thwarted nature, of discontinuity between present and past, Ashbery has turned his agitation into a principle of composition. From the start he has looked for sentences, diction, a syntax which would make these feelings fully and fluidly available. When he used strict verse forms, as he did in much of his first book, *Some Trees*, it was always with a sense of their power to explore rather than to certify that he was a poet. There are three sestinas in *Some Trees*, and one, the remarkable "Faust," in his second book, *The Tennis Court Oath*.

> These forms such as the sestina were really devices at getting into remoter areas of consciousness. The really bizarre requirements of a sestina I use as a probing tool. . . . I once told somebody that writing a sestina was rather like riding downhill on a bicycle and having the pedals push your feet. I wanted my feet to be pushed into places they wouldn't normally have taken. . . .[4]

Ashbery's rhyming, too, was restless. At the close of "Some Trees" his final rhymes create a practically unparaphraseable meaning, the two words inviting overtones they wouldn't have in prose:

> Placed in a puzzling light, and moving,
> Our days put on such reticence
> These accents seem their own defense.

There were other, drastic attempts to get at "remoter areas of consciousness," some of them in *The Tennis Court Oath* close to automatic writing. "Europe," a poem Ashbery now thinks of as a dead end, was "a way of trying to obliterate the poetry that at the time was coming naturally"[5] to him. Exploding any notion of continuity, it consisted of "a lot of splintered fragments . . . collecting them all under a series of numbers." The "French Poems" in *The Double Dream of Spring* were first written in French, then translated "with the idea of avoiding customary word-patterns and associations."[6] In *Three Poems*, his fifth book, long prose pieces were a way to overflow the "arbitrary divisions of poetry into lines," another way to an "expanded means of utterance."[7]

What I am getting at is that a great deal of Ashbery's writing is done in an atmosphere of deliberate demolition, and that his work is best served not by thinking about development, but by following his own advice: beginning at the beginning, "that is, the present." *Self-Portrait in a Convex Mirror* (1975) is the present with which I want to begin. The long title poem of that volume is in every sense a major work, a strong and beautiful resolution of besetting and important problems. Ashbery had already broached these problems in *The Double Dream of Spring*, in which he characteristically approached the world as a foreigner, sometimes in the role of explorer, sometimes as a pilgrim, and almost always as someone bewildered by the clutter of a situation which, wryly phrased, "could not be better." The world of that book is often divided, out of bristling necessity, between inside and outside, between *we* and a dimly identified *they*, as in "The Task": "They are preparing to begin again: / Problems, new pennant up the flagpole / In a predicated romance." Access to the present was more peremptorily barred than it was to be in *Self-Portrait in a Convex Mirror*.

The Double Dream of Spring had looked at alternatives with grim amusement. In "Definition of Blue" the cant words of social engineers, historians and broadcasters—*capitalism, romanticism, impetuses*—drain away, with their tripping rhythms, into colorless sentences, while the imaginative eye, seeking out materials for escape, finds only that "erosion" has produced:

> a kind of dust or exaggerated pumice
> Which fills space and transforms it, becoming a medium
> In which it is possible to recognize oneself.

This comic decay of language and the laws of perspective allows us "A portrait, smooth as glass, . . . built up out of multiple corrections / And it has no relation to the space or time in which it was lived." The joke is on us, especially the grammatical joke that it is the portrait which lives, fragments of personality out of touch with anything but the mirroring tricks which make it seem to be a likeness. Meanwhile

> the blue surroundings drift slowly up and past you
> To realize themselves some day, while, you, in this nether
> world that could not be better

> Waken each morning to the exact value of what you did and
>   said, which remains.

The separation of "nether world" from the independent and in-accessible world of plenitude, the blue surroundings which drift past us and "realize themselves," is a source of frustration and mockery.

> There is no remedy for this "packaging" which has
>   supplanted the old sensations.
> Formerly there would have been architectural screens at the
>   point where the action became most difficult

Yet Ashbery also takes a rueful "pop" pleasure in the vocabulary of "packaging," allowing it to deflate itself, as in the double-take of a "world that could not be better." The feelings here are not totally resolved, nor are they meant to be. Ashbery once said that he was willing for his poems to be "confusing, but not confused."

> It seems to me that my poetry sometimes proceeds as though an argument were suddenly derailed and something that started out clearly suddenly becomes opaque. It's a kind of mimesis of how experience comes to me: as one is listening to someone else—a lecturer, for instance—who's making perfect sense but suddenly slides into something that eludes one. What I am probably trying to do is to illustrate opacity and how it can suddenly descend over us, rather than trying to be willfully obscure.[8]

"Definition of Blue" is, on the surface, laconically faithful to expository syntax, the *sinces* and *buts* and *therefores* which lash explanations together. The logical bridges lead into eroded territory, and then unexpectedly back again; the poem moves in and out of focus like a mind bombarded with received ideas. So—"mass practices have sought to submerge the personality / By ignoring it, which has caused it instead to branch out in all directions." Or, with deadpan determination—"there is no point in looking to imaginative new methods / Since all of them are in constant use." Just at the point when imagination seems reduced to novelty, an overloaded switchboard, we learn that this "erosion" with its "kind of dust or exaggerated pumice" provides "a medium / In which it is possible to recognize onself." A serious challenge peeps through: how far are we responsible for, dependent upon, these denatured senses of identity?

"Each new diversion," Ashbery tells us, "adds its accurate touch to the ensemble." Mischievous saboteur that he is, Ashbery's pun on *diversion* shows how much he enjoys some of the meandering of unfocused public vocabularies and the "accurate touches" they supply (as a wardrobe?). But, basically, our sense is of someone bristling, boxed in by a maze of idioms, frustrated and diminished by his presence there. Only the mirrored portrait lives "built up out of multiple corrections." Or, to be more exact, in a petrifying shift to a past tense and the passive voice: "it has no relation to the space or time in which it was lived"—a disaffected vision of personality if there ever was one. The world of "packaging" appears to have robbed him of a life, of his access to power and vision.

I have chosen this example, more extreme than some of the others in *The Double Dream of Spring*, because it is so energetically answered and refigured by Ashbery's long poem "Self-Portrait in a Convex Mirror." In that more recent, more encompassing work, the poet takes charge of the emerging self-portrait rather than suffering it as he had in "Definition of Blue." He tests an identity captured by art against the barrages of experience which nourish and beset it. He is sparked by a Renaissance painting, Parmigianino's self-portrait, alongside which he matches what proves to be his own: a mirror of the state of mind in which the poem was written, open to waves of discovery and distraction, and aware of the unframed and unframeable nature of experience:

> Today has no margins, the event arrives
> Flush with its edges, is of the same substance,
> Indistinguishable.

Parmigianino's work is itself problematic and haunting, done on the segment of a halved wooden ball so as to reproduce as closely as possible the painter's image in a convex mirror exactly the same size. That Renaissance effort, straining to capture a real presence, touches off in Ashbery a whirling series of responses, visions and revisions of what the painting asks of *him*.

1

"Self-Portrait" begins quietly, not overcommitted to its occasion, postponing full sentences, preferring phrases:

> As Parmigianino did it, the right hand
> Bigger than the head, thrust at the viewer
> And swerving easily away, as though to protect
> What it advertises. A few leaded panes, old beams,
> Fur, pleated muslin, a coral ring rung together
> In a movement supporting the face, which swims
> Toward and away like the hand
> Except that it is in repose. It is what is
> Sequestered.
>
> (68)*

A lot could be said about Ashbery's entrance into poems and his habit of tentative anchorage: "As on a festal day in early spring," "As One Put Drunk into the Packet Boat" (title: first line of Marvell's "Tom May's Death"). Such openings are reticent, similes taking on the identity of another occasion, another person—a sideways address to their subject or, in the case of "Self-Portrait," a way of dealing with temptation. The speaker in "Self-Portrait" appears to "happen" upon Parmigianino's painting as a solution to a problem pondered before the poem begins. At first glimpse the glass of art and the face in the portrait offer him just the right degree of self-disclosure and self-assertion, the right balance of living spirit and the haunting concentrated maneuvers of art. The judicious give-and-take appeals to him: thrust and swerve; toward and away; protect and advertise. (This is, by the way, one of the best descriptive impressions of a painting I know.) That balanced

---

* Numerals in parentheses refer to page numbers in *Self-Portrait in a Convex Mirror*.

satisfaction never returns. What at first comforts him, the face "in repose," prompts an unsettling fear: "It is what is / Sequestered." This is the first full sentence of the poem—brief, shocked and considered, after the glancing descriptive phrases. An earlier draft of the lines was weaker: "protected" rather than "sequestered" and the word placed unemphatically at the end of the line, as if some of the menace to be sensed in the finished portrait hadn't yet surfaced.

From then on the poem becomes, as Ashbery explains it in a crucial pun, "speculation / (From the Latin *speculum*, mirror),", Ashbery's glass rather than Francesco's. All questions of scientific reflection, capturing a real presence, turn instantly into the other kind of reflection: changeable, even fickle thought. The whole poem is a series of revisions prepared for in the opening lines, where in Parmigianino's receding portrait he imagines first that "the soul establishes itself," then that "the soul is a captive." Finally, from the portrait's mixture of "tenderness, amusement and regret":

> The secret is too plain. The pity of it smarts,
> Makes hot tears spurt: that the soul is not a soul,
> Has no secret, is small, and it fits
> Its hollow perfectly: its room, our moment of attention.
>
> (69)

In an earlier draft of the poem it was not quite so clear why such strong feeling emerges:

> that the soul
> Has no secret, is small, though it fits
> Perfectly the space intended for it: its room, our attention.

Rewriting those lines Ashbery allowed more emphatic fears to surface. "The soul is not a soul." Acting on an earlier hint that Parmigianino's mirror chose to show an image "glazed, embalmed," Ashbery sees it in its hollow (overtones of burial) rather than in the neutral "space intended." "Our moment of attention" draws sparks between the glazed surface of the portrait and the poet's transient interest which awakens it, and places notions like the *soul* irredeemably in the eye of the beholder. When the poet looks at this ghostly double, alive in its mirroring appeal, the emerging fear comes across like Milly Theale's (*The Wings of the Dove*) in front of the Bronzino portrait resembling her, "dead, dead, dead."

Throughout "Self-Portrait in a Convex Mirror" the poet speaks to the portrait as in easy consultation with a familiar, but with an ever changing sense of whether he is addressing the image, trapped on its wooden globe, or addressing the free painter standing outside his creation, straining to capture a real presence, restraining the power to shatter what may become a prison: "Francesco, your hand is big enough / To wreck the sphere, . . ." An explosion has been building from the start as Ashbery returns over and over, puzzled by that hand which the convex mirror shows "Bigger than the head, thrust at the viewer / And swerving easily away, as though to protect / What it advertises." At first that defensive posture in a work of art attracts him, an icon of mastery. But, a little later, feeling the portrait as "life englobed," he reads the hand differently:

> One would like to stick one's hand
> Out of the globe, but its dimension,
> What carries it, will not allow it.
> No doubt it is this, not the reflex
> To hide something, which makes the hand loom large
> As it retreats slightly.

The hand returns not in self-defense, but

> to fence in and shore up the face
> On which the effort of this condition reads
> Like a pinpoint of a smile, a spark
> Or star one is not sure of having seen
> As darkness resumes.

(69-70)

Philosophic questions mount, but always apprehended through gestures, new expressions glimpsed as one stares at the painting—here a glint of self-mockery, as the painter absorbed with prowess finds himself trapped by his medium after all. "But your eyes proclaim / That everything is surface. . . . / There are no recesses in the room, only alcoves." The window admits light, but all sense of change is excluded, even "the weather, which in French is / *Le temps*, the word for time." The opening section of "Self-Portrait" winds down, the poet bemused but his poetry drained of the emotional concentration which had drawn him to the painting; a glance at the subject's hands sees them as symbolically placed, but inexpressive:

> The whole is stable within
> Instability, a globe like ours, resting
> On a pedestal of vacuum, a ping-pong ball
> Secure on its jet of water.
> And just as there are no words for the surface, that is,
> No words to say what it really is, that it is not
> Superficial but a visible core, then there is
> No way out of the problem of pathos vs. experience.
> You will stay on, restive, serene in
> Your gesture which is neither embrace nor warning
> But which holds something of both in pure
> Affirmation that doesn't affirm anything.
>
> (70)

This is not Ashbery's final reading of the portrait's gesturing hand. But it launches a series of struggles with the past, with "art," with the notion of "surface," with the random demands of the present—struggles which are not only at the heart of this poem but a paradigm of Ashbery's work. Parmigianino's portrait has to compete with the furniture of the mind confronting it: the poet's day, memories, surroundings, ambitions, distractions. The solid spherical segment becomes confused, in the Wonderland of the mind, with other rounded images, toys of attention—a ping-pong ball on a jet of water, and then, at the start of the second section, "The balloon pops, the attention / Turns dully away." There is a rhythm to reading this poem, however wandering it may seem. We experience it as a series of contractions and expansions of interest in the painting, depending upon how much the poet is drawn to its powers of foreshortening and concentration, and alternately how cramped he feels breathing its air. The transitions between sections are marked as easy shifts in inner weather, opposed to the weatherless chamber of Parmigianino's portrait:

> The balloon pops, the attention
> Turns dully away.
> . . . .
> As I start to forget it
> It presents its stereotype again
> . . . .
> The shadow of the city injects its own
> Urgency:
> . . . .
> A breeze like the turning of a page
> Brings back your face.

The painting occurs to him at times as a ship: first, a "tiny, self-important ship / On the surface." In mysterious relation to it the enlarged hand in the distorted portrait seems "Like a dozing whale on the sea bottom." Threatening? Or a sign of throbbing vitality, an invisible part of its world? Later the portrait

> is an unfamiliar stereotype, the face
> Riding at anchor, issued from hazards, soon
> To accost others, "rather angel than man" (Vasari).
> (73)

Toward the end of the poem, the ship sails in to confirm some sense of

> this otherness
> That gets included in the most ordinary
> Forms of daily activity, changing everything
> Slightly and profoundly, and tearing the matter
> Of creation, any creation, not just artistic creation
> Out of our hands, to install it on some monstrous, near
> Peak, too close to ignore, too far
> For one to intervene? This otherness, this
> "Not-being-us" is all there is to look at
> In the mirror, though no one can say

> How it came to be this way. A ship
> Flying unknown colors has entered the harbor.
>
> (81)

Self-important and tiny? Issued from hazards? Flying unknown
colors? Through contradictory senses of the ship, Ashbery judges
the portrait's relation to risk and adventure, to the mysterious
otherness of "arrival" in a completed work of art.

What happens, for example, when we start to imagine the life
of cities behind the surface of a work of art, in this case the sack
of Rome which was going on where Francesco was at work; Vienna
where Ashbery saw the painting in 1959; New York where he is
writing his poem? These are ways Ashbery has of summoning up
the countless events which nourished the painting and his response
to it. That outside life, again imagined in terms of risk, adventure,
voyages, can be profoundly disturbing—a life not palpable in a
"finished" work.

> a chill, a blight
> Moving outward along the capes and peninsulas
> Of your nervures and so to the archipelagoes
> And to the bathed, aired secrecy of the open sea.
>
> (75)

Such images focus the problem of how much life is lived in and
outside a work of art. There is no point in disentangling what is
hopelessly intertwined. The images flow toward and counter one
another, and the reader accumulates a bewildering sense of what
it is to be both fulfilled and thwarted by his own grasped moments
of vision (all attempts at order, not just artistic creation, Ashbery
tries to remind us). Francesco's portrait has the capacity to make
us feel at home; we "can live in it as in fact we have done." Or
"we linger, receiving / Dreams and inspirations on an unassigned /
Frequency." But at another moment the portrait seems like a
vacuum drawing upon *our* plenty, "fed by our dreams." If at one
point the mind straying from the conical painting is like a balloon
bursting, not much later the straying thoughts are imagined as
wayward, even sinister progeny of the painting: the balloon has

not burst at all. "Actually / The skin of the bubble-chamber's as tough as / Reptile eggs."

Struggling with the past, with art and its completeness, Ashbery is also struggling with the impulses behind his own writing at the very moment of writing.

> you could be fooled for a moment
> Before you realize the reflection
> Isn't yours. You feel then like one of those
> Hoffmann characters who have been deprived
> Of a reflection, except that the whole of me
> Is seen to be supplanted by the strict
> Otherness of the painter in his
> Other room.
>
> (74)

The threat is pressed home by a shift from an impersonal "you" to an endangered "me." The finished work of art is like "A cloth over a birdcage," and the poet wary of its invitations:

> Yet the "poetic," straw-colored space
> Of the long corridor that leads back to the painting,
> Its darkening opposite—is this
> Some figment of "art," not to be imagined
> As real, let alone special?
>
> (77-78)

By the closing pages of the poem two irreconcilable views of "living" have proposed themselves. Parmigianino's appears to be a "Life-obstructing task." ("You can't live there.") More than that, the portrait exposes the poet's own efforts in the present:

> Our time gets to be veiled, compromised
> By the portrait's will to endure. It hints at
> Our own, which we were hoping to keep hidden.
>
> (79-80)

When "will to endure" and "life-obstructing" are identified with one another, as they are here in describing our daily fiction-making activities, the psychological contradictions are themselves almost unendurable. Imagining is as alien and miraculous as the ambivalent image he finds for it: "A ship / Flying unknown colors has entered the harbor." Our creations, torn out of our hands, seem installed "on some monstrous, near / Peak, too close to ignore, too far / For one to intervene." Another way of looking at it: "the way of telling" intrudes "as in the game where / A whispered phrase passed around the room / Ends up as something completely different."

An alternative? Though the poem is always pressing us out of the past, it has no unmediated language for the present, which is as hard to locate as other poets' Edens. Where poets describing unknown worlds have always "liken'd spiritual forms to corporal," Ashbery must perform some of the same *likening* to enter the corporal present itself. He knows the present only from before and after, seen as through a terrifying hourglass:

> the sands are hissing
> As they approach the beginning of the big slide
> Into what happened. This past
> Is now here.

(81)

Four of these five monosyllables—"This past is now here"—point to the present with all the immediacy of which English is capable, and *past* disarms them all. There is no comfort in the provisional, in being open to the rush of things. In fact, one of the most devastating contemporary critiques of randomness in poetry comes in the final moments of Ashbery's poem. Yet it is a critique from within, in a poem open to the vagaries of mind—and from a writer deeply committed to describing the struggles we undergo in describing our lives. This is his unique and special place among contemporary poets. The blurring of personal pronouns, their often indeterminate reference, the clouding of landscapes and crystal balls, are all ways of trying to be true not only to the mind's confusions but also to its resistance of stiffening formulations.

In the distorting self-portrait of Parmigianino, Ashbery found the perfect mirror and the perfect antagonist—a totem of art and the past caught in the act of trying to escape from itself. Parmigia-

nino's work of art confirms the poet in a vocation which refuses
to be rescued by art, except in the moment of creation.

> Hasn't it too its lair
> In the present we are always escaping from
> And falling back into, as the waterwheel of days
> Pursues its uneventful, even serene course?
>
> (78-79)

This is a difficult dialectic to which he submits. Francesco is the
indispensable partner in a continuing conversation; yet Ashbery's
final reading of the painterly hand in the self-portrait is the boldest
stroke of all:

> Therefore I beseech you, withdraw that hand,
> Offer it no longer as shield or greeting,
> The shield of a greeting, Francesco:
> There is room for one bullet in the chamber:
> Our looking through the wrong end
> Of the telescope as you fall back at a speed
> Faster than that of light to flatten ultimately
> Among the features of the room, . . .
>
> (82)

The pun on *chamber*, the dizzying transformations of rounded
room into telescope and gun barrel, are triumphant tributes to all
the contradictions of this poem and the hard-won struggle to be
free of them. It would be a shallow reading which sees this poem
as a modernist's dismissal of the past. Ashbery translates that
topos into radical and embracing human terms. The elation we
feel comes from the writer's own unwillingness to take permanent
shelter in his work. Any work of art—not just those of the distant
past—has designs on us, exposes for what it is our "will to endure."
Ashbery builds the awareness of death and change into the very
form of his work. It is the old subject of Romantic lyric—of
Keats's *Ode on a Grecian Urn*—but here without undue veneration
for the moments out of time. Ashbery admits into the interstices
of his poem a great deal of experience—confusion, comedy, be-
fuddlement, preoccupation—in which he takes as much joy as in

the "cold pockets / Of remembrance, whispers out of time," which he also celebrates. His withdrawal from the privileged moments is never as regretful or as final as Keats's from his "cold pastoral." Nor is it as rueful as Ashbery's own sense of desertion in "Definition of Blue" where "you, in this nether world that could not be better / Waken each morning to the exact value of what you did and said, which remains." In that earlier poem Ashbery feels diminished and powerless before a "portrait, smooth as glass, . . . built up out of multiple corrections," which "has no relation to the space or time in which it was lived." In the spaciousness of "Self-Portrait in a Convex Mirror" Ashbery radiates a new confidence in his ability to accommodate what is in the poet's mind: the concentrated poem and its teeming surroundings. In its achieved generosity and fluidity, in its stops and starts and turns, Ashbery's long poem dispels some of the frustrations of language and form, or assimilates them more closely into the anxieties and frustrations of living.

2

I said before that "Self-Portrait in a Convex Mirror" answers problems posed by Ashbery's poetic past and helps refigure it.

> Every moment is surrounded by a lot of things in life that don't add up to anything that makes much sense and these are part of a situation that I feel I'm trying to deal with when I'm writing.[9]

Ashbery said this to an interviewer in 1972, as if anticipating the free and flexible voice he found for "Self-Portrait in a Convex Mirror." That year he had published the long prose pieces he entitled *Three Poems*, a work which evidently released him into an "expanded sense of utterance":

> . . . the idea of it occurred to me as something new in which the arbitrary divisions of poetry into lines would get abolished. One wouldn't have to have these interfering and scanning the processes of one's thought as one was writing; the poetic form would be dissolved, in solution, and therefore

> create a much more—I hate to say environmental because it's
> a bad word—but more of a surrounding thing like the way
> one's consciousness is surrounded by one's thoughts.[10]

However odd or puzzling that last phrase may be, we can sense
the pressure behind its deliberate, almost involuntary awkwardness.
In both quotations Ashbery uses the word "surrounded" to suggest
the number of seemingly unrelated "thoughts" or "things" at any
given moment pressing behind the little that is articulated. This
tension is the point of departure for *Three Poems*:

> I thought that if I could put it all down, that would be one
> way. And next the thought came to me that to leave all out
> would be another, and truer, way.
>
>   clean-washed sea
>   The flowers were.
>
> These are examples of leaving out. But, forget as we will,
> something soon comes to stand in their place. Not the truth,
> perhaps, but—yourself. It is you who made this, therefore you
> are true.

We are dealing with rich polarities in Ashbery's work. The impulse to "leave all out" can be felt as early as a poem like "Illustration" from his first book, *Some Trees*. The protagonist of that
poem is a nun about to leave behind the irrelevancies of the world
by leaping from a skyscraper. As this droll hierophant remarks:
" 'I desire / Monuments. . . . I want to move / Figuratively, as
waves caress / The thoughtless shore.' " The narrator, too, is convinced: "Much that is beautiful must be discarded / So that we
may resemble a taller / Impression of ourselves." That was one
way of saying it, the way of concision and foreshortening.

But then there is another way to have it, as in "And *Ut Pictura
Poesis* Is Her Name," a more recent poem (1975):

> You can't say it that way any more.
> Bothered about beauty you have to
> Come out into the open, into a clearing,
> And rest. . . .

Now
About what to put in your poem-painting:
Flowers are always nice, particularly delphinium.
Names of boys you once knew and their sleds,
Skyrockets are good—do they still exist?
There are a lot of other things of the same quality
As those I've mentioned. Now one must
Find a few important words, and a lot of low-keyed,
Dull-sounding ones.

A difference in approach makes all the difference. "Illustration" proposes a "taller / Impression of ourselves," an epigrammatic and visionary avoidance of ordinary "beauty," "*Ut Pictura*" makes space for a flustered, fuller and meandering version of self. Vision is invited by coming out into a clearing and taking a relaxed view of the surroundings. The poet finds "a few important words" and "a lot of low-keyed, / Dull-sounding ones."

Though these poems come from different periods in Ashbery's career, I don't want to suggest that one voice or approach replaces the other. But with *Three Poems* Ashbery rounded a critical corner. Its *perpetuum mobile* style prepared him, when he returned to verse, for a new fluidity, a way to re-admit the self to his poetry. Alive in its present, and determined as a Jack-in-the-Box, that self pops up when any moment of poetic concision threatens to falsify or obliterate it. The discovery comes as a relief, not so much a calculation as a necessity. Leaving things out, "forget as we will, something soon comes to stand in their place. Not the truth, perhaps, but—yourself."

I am talking, then, about complementary gifts or voices in Ashbery's poetry. He has his own deadpan way of putting it: "In the last few years I have been attempting to keep meaningfulness up to the pace of randomness . . . but I really think that meaningfulness can't get along without randomness and that they somehow have to be brought together."[11] No wonder that the long "Self-Portrait in a Convex Mirror" stands as a centerpiece to his work in the early 1970s; no single short poem could handle such a copious problem. It would be a mistake to see this merely as an aesthetic question, a poet talking about poetry, about the relative virtues of condensed vision and expansive randomness. The emotional coloring that Ashbery gives this conflict, especially in his long poem, suggests psychological dimensions and stresses. Art "leaving things out" involves a sense of melancholy and sacrifice, a restlessness, a threat to vitality.

The Double Dream of Spring is shadowed by such feelings; the short poems of *Self-Portrait in a Convex Mirror* often counter them. Together these two books, five years apart, with their different moods, give a sense of the range and playfulness and boldness of Ashbery's emerging work. There are some poems, of course, which might be in either book. Still, certain characteristic titles belong to one and not the other: in *Double Dream*, "Spring Day," "Summer," "Evening in the Country," "Rural Objects," "Clouds"; in *Self-Portrait*, "Worsening Situation," "Absolute Clearance," "Mixed Feelings," "No Way of Knowing," "All and Some." The latter pick up colloquial ways of describing the emotional weather of the moment. Titles from *Double Dream* tend toward the generic and the pastoral. (Not that any Ashbery title is more than a clue or a point of departure, less a summary and more a key signature for the poem.)

In *The Double Dream of Spring* Ashbery seems absorbed in the forms that lie just behind an experience; the day's events, in "Years of Indiscretion," are "Fables that time invents / To explain its passing." Common phrases are challenged; buried meanings are coaxed out of them so that they surprise us with a life of their own, or chastise us for a sleepy acceptance of the "phraseology we become." Ashbery wants to push past the hardening of life into habit, the way it congeals into patterned phrases, the metaphysician's equivalent of "You are what you eat." I don't know whether "Young Man with Letter" is touched off by yet another appearance of a golden, well-introduced youth into the city which will absorb him. But the impulse of the poem quickly becomes something else: to awaken the "fable" sleeping behind a phrase like "making the rounds."

Another feeble, wonderful creature is making the rounds again,
In this phraseology we become, as clouds like leaves
Fashion the internal structure of a season
From water into ice. Such an abstract can be
Dazed waking of the words with no memory of what happened before,
Waiting for the second click. We know them well enough now,
Forever, from living into them, tender, frivolous and puzzled
And we know that with them we will come out right.

The cliché ("making the rounds") is teased alive by the strange sad comparison with the seasons. Ashbery performs what he then identifies, "dazed waking of the words," eventually "living into them." Many of the poems in *Double Dream* act out such discoveries, satisfied with nothing merely accidental, nothing less refined than "Fables that time invents / To explain its passing." Still, having gone beyond gossip in "Young Man with Letter," having absorbed a single bit of tattle into a large melancholy sense of natural cycles, Ashbery is left with some nagging questions. Once he has sidestepped the "corrosive friends" and "quiet bickering" in this poem, there is still something distant and unreal about the "straining and puffing / . . . commas produce":

> Is it not more likely that . . .
> . . .   this ferment
> We take as suddenly our present
> Is our waltzing somewhere else, down toward the view
> But holding off?

The frustration and self-mockery, the sense of being deprived of the present, are inescapably twinned with the discoveries made in such poems. The mood is odd and disquieting; however gratifying the visionary insight, the poet also seems to feel experience being taken out of his hands. Hence, the way fresh hopes verge into nightmares in the long suspended sentence at the opening of "Spring Day":

> The immense hope, and forbearance
> Trailing out of night, to sidewalks of the day
> Like air breathed into a paper city, exhaled
> As night returns bringing doubts

> That swarm around the sleeper's head
> But are fended off with clubs and knives, so that morning
> Installs again in cold hope
> The air that was yesterday, is what you are.

In this supple maze of syntax things seem over, exhausted, before they begin; "immense hope" turns into "cold hope" in "the air that was yesterday."

Again, a sense of pleasure in natural cycles is slowly withdrawn in "Years of Indiscretion."

> Whatever your eye alights on this morning is yours:
> Dotted rhythms of colors as they fade to the color,
> A gray agate, translucent and firm, with nothing
> Beyond its purifying reach. It's all there.
> These are things offered to your participation.
>
> These pebbles in a row are the seasons.
> This is a house in which you may wish to live.
> There are more than any of us to choose from
> But each must live its own time.

The experience offered here, beginning in random pleasures of the eye, seems at first to belong to us, to *our* wishes and choices. And yet "participation" suggests limits to our control, and the ambiguous "its" in the last line shadows independent processes in which we "participate" but do not endure. The grave diction soon removes us into an atmosphere refined and impersonal, our lives roles rather than improvisations. "There ought to be room for more things, for a spreading out, like," Ashbery says of the generalizing screen which stands between us and details of the landscape ("For John Clare"). "Alas, we perceive them if at all as those things that were meant to be put aside—costumes of the supporting actors or voice trilling at the end of a narrow enclosed street."

In one of his best short poems, "Summer," Ashbery imagines the winter latent in summer branches: "For the time being the shadow is ample / And hardly seen, divided among the twigs of a tree." Winter's poverty emerges later in a full-blown reminiscence of Stevens: "and winter, the twitter / Of cold stars at the pane, that describes with broad gestures / This state of being that is not so big after all." I am struck by the frequency with which Ashbery returns in *Double Dream* to myths of the seasons, as to photographic negatives, for the true contours governing experience—and what's more important, he is looking not for myths of rebirth but for myths of diminution. In "Fragment" we learn that

> Summer was a band of nondescript children
> Bordering the picture of winter, which was indistinct
> And gray like the sky of a winter afternoon.

In the poem "Summer," "Summer involves going down as a steep flight of steps / To a narrow ledge over the water."

Ashbery takes his title *The Double Dream of Spring* from de Chirico and so puts us on warning that we are stepping through the looking glass into those deep perspectives and receding landscapes of the mind. He leads us, once we are prepared to follow, to yearned-for, difficult states, free of casual distraction.

> To reduce all this to a small variant,
> To step free at last, minuscule on the gigantic plateau—
> This was our ambition: to be small and clear and free.
> ("Soonest Mended")

Does the present exist principally "To release the importance / Of what will always remain invisible?" he asks, with some urgency, in "Fragment." *The Double Dream of Spring* seems to answer that question in the affirmative. It is Ashbery's most successfully visionary book, however sad its tone. Unlike *Self-Portrait in a Convex Mirror*, which struggles to include and authenticate the present, *Double Dream* finds the most striking images in its glimpses of the fables behind our lives, and it most yearns for the state which is both free and deathlike, diminished.

> The welcoming stuns the heart, iron bells
> Crash through the transparent metal of the sky
> Each day slowing the method of thought a little
> Until oozing sap of touchable mortality, time lost and won.

"Soonest Mended"—so goes the title of one of the best of these poems, illustrating a point we can scarcely grasp until we supply the first half of a proverb which has been mimetically suppressed: "least said; soonest mended." *Double Dream* calls for tight-lipped irony as well as yearning for visionary release. In "Soonest Mended" comic self-awareness and proverbial wisdom are the ways Ashbery finds to deal with the deposits of history and hazard which determine the course of life:

> They were the players, and we who had struggled at the game
> Were merely spectators, though subject to its vicissitudes
> And moving with it out of the tearful stadium, borne on
>   shoulders, at last.

It is entirely in keeping with the tone of this poem that we are left uncertain as to whether we are borne out of the stadium triumphant or dead. Or both. Just as, at the end of "Soonest Mended," action is described as

>   this careless
> Preparing, sowing the seeds crooked in the furrow,
> Making ready to forget, and always coming back
> To the mooring of starting out, that day so long ago.

The brave carelessness here is licensed by some certainty that no matter how many mistakes we make, no matter what happens, we *do* return to the "mooring of starting out." We can also read this as helplessness. The tone is partly elegiac, owning up to the futility of our efforts, with "mooring" sounding as much like death as a new life. The entire poem has this doubleness of feeling. Its long breathy lines shift quickly from one historical hazard to another; it doesn't take long to get from the endangered Angelica of Ariosto and Ingres to Happy Hooligan in his rusted green automobile. Caught up in a whirligig of historical process, the self has no chance to recover balance, and above all, no conceptual means, no language to do so. Still, the energetic lines breathe the *desire* to assert ego and vitality. The poem sees the world as so full of bright particulars that no rules of thumb can keep up with them; and so it is fairly bitter about standard patterns of history and learning, sees them only as shaky hypotheses. "Soonest Mended" doesn't yet pretend pleasure in the present, a pleasure Ashbery *does* experience in later poems; and yet the poem doesn't entirely fall back on dreams of another world. Falling back, not with too much conviction, on the proverbial wisdom of the title, Ashbery has found a middle diction: ready to improvise, yielding to but not swamped by randomness.

3

I have talked about complementary voices and attitudes in Ashbery's work—alternatives between which "Soonest Mended" seems poised—the ways of concision and copiousness. Before *Three Poems* Ashbery was strongly attracted to foreshortening, "leaving all out," moving figuratively: discarding things so that we "resemble a taller / Impression of ourselves." It is easy to forget how fierce and compelling that desire was:

> groping shadows of an incomplete
> Former existence so close it burns like the mouth that
> Closes down over all your effort like the moment
> Of death, but stays, raging and burning the design of
> Its intentions into the house of your brain, until
> You wake up alone, the certainty that it
> Wasn't a dream your only clue to why the walls
> Are turning on you and why the windows no longer speak
> Of time but are themselves, transparent guardians you
> Invented for what there was to hide.

Something has happened between that fevered vision from "Clepsydra" and the more relaxed, but still yearning, close of "Self-Portrait in a Convex Mirror": the Parmigianino portrait recedes, virtually assassinated by the poet; it becomes

> an invitation
> Never mailed, the "it was all a dream"
> Syndrome, though the "all" tells tersely
> Enough how it wasn't. Its existence
> Was real, though troubled, and the ache

> Of this waking dream can never drown out
> The diagram still sketched on the wind,
> Chosen, meant for me and materialized
> In the disguising radiance of my room.

Both this passage and the one from "Clepsydra" acknowledge a constellation of dreams perhaps more "real" than "real life" ("the certainty that it / Wasn't a dream"). But the version in "Self-Portrait" is wistful, rather than driven: Ashbery seems open to the varieties of experience, registers more pleasurably the ache of the veiled and ineluctable dream. He makes his bow to an ironic view of the visionary self ("the 'it was all a dream' / Syndrome") before returning to a hidden truth behind colloquial language ("the 'all' tells tersely / Enough how it wasn't"). The present *disguises* the tempting dream behind Parmigianino's portrait, but disguises it in the "radiance" of the poet's room. No need to choose between the present and the unseen—and in the pressured light of the passing of time, no *way* to do so.

It is the jumble of everyday pleasures and frustrations that we hear most often in the fluid style of some of the shorter poems of *Self-Portrait in a Convex Mirror*. Even the longer poem "Grand Galop" is almost literally an attempt to keep the poem's accounting powers even with the pace of inner and outer events. Naturally it doesn't succeed. The mind moves in several directions at once, and the poem is partly about the exhaustions and comic waste carried along by the "stream of consciousness":

> The custard is setting; meanwhile
> I not only have my own history to worry about
> But am forced to fret over insufficient details related to large
> Unfinished concepts that can never bring themselves to the point
> Of being, with or without my help, if any were forthcoming.

At the start of the poem, the mind moves on ahead of some lists of names (weigela, sloppy joe on bun—the end of the line for Whitman's famous catalogues) and then the poem says we must stop and "wait again." "Nothing takes up its fair share of time."

Ashbery calls our attention repeatedly, and with frustration rather than exultation, to the fact that the poem's time is not actual time.

"Grand Galop" also laments the generalizing and pattern-making powers which intervene and block our experience of particulars:

> Too bad, I mean, that getting to know each just for a
>   fleeting second
> Must be replaced by imperfect knowledge of the featureless
>   whole,
> Like some pocket history of the world, so general
> As to constitute a sob or wail unrelated
> To any attempt at definition.

Imperfect and *featureless* fall with deadpan accuracy in lines which expose the hazards of "aping naturalness." Ashbery's "A Man of Words" finds that

> All diaries are alike, clear and cold, with
> The outlook for continued cold. They are placed
> Horizontal, parallel to the earth,
> Like the unencumbering dead. Just time to reread this
> And the past slips through your fingers, wishing you were there.

Poetry can never be quite quick enough, however grand the "galop," however strong the desire to "communicate something between breaths." This explains some of the qualities of Ashbery's style which trouble readers. What seems strange is not so much *what* he says as the space between his sentences, the quickness of his transitions. "He" will become "you" or "I" without warning as experiences move close and then farther away, photographs and tapes of themselves. Tenses will shift while the poem refers to itself as part of the past. We feel as if something were missing; we become anxious as if a step had been skipped. So does the poet who, in several of the shorter poems, describes himself as a dazed prologue to someone else's play. In "As One Put Drunk into the Packet Boat," he longs for a beautiful apocalypse:

> for a moment, I thought
> The great, formal affair was beginning, orchestrated,
> Its colors concentrated in a glance, a ballade

That takes in the whole world, now, but lightly,
Still lightly, but with wide authority and tact.

There are moments when Ashbery takes perilous shelter in the
world of fable and dream, as in "Hop o' My Thumb," whose
speaker, a kind of Bluebeard, imagines possessing his sirens ("The
necklace of wishes alive and breathing around your throat") in an
atmosphere at once hothouse and *Lost Horizon:*

There are still other made-up countries
Where we can hide forever,
Wasted with eternal desire and sadness,
Sucking the sherbets, crooning the tunes, naming the names.

Yet these worlds, while drawing out some gorgeous imaginings,
generate as much restlessness as the confusing world of daytime
plenty. We may share the moment in "Märchenbilder" when
"One of those lovelorn sonatas / For wind instruments was riding
past on a solemn white horse." With it goes impatience, the desire to escape, a very rich and suggestive ambivalence. The fairy
tales

are empty as cupboards.
To spend whole days drenched in them, waiting for the next
    whisper,
For the word in the next room. This is how the princes must
    have behaved,
Lying down in the frugality of sleep.

The third of the exotic poems in this volume, "Scheherazade," suggests what Ashbery is after in such works. He doesn't retell the
story of the Sultan and the ideal storyteller, but he does explore
with evident interest and desire the condition of that inventive
lady. She is part of a world of dry lands, beneath which are rich
hidden springs. "An inexhaustible wardrobe has been placed at the
disposal / Of each new occurrence." She loves the "colored verbs
and adjectives,"

But most of all she loved the particles
That transform objects of the same category

> Into particular ones, each distinct
> Within and apart from its own class.
> In all this springing up was no hint
> Of a tide, only a pleasant wavering of the air
> In which all things seemed present.

That love of detail and rich ability to cope with it, an experience of the world without anxiety, without being overwhelmed by plenitude, is rarely felt in *Self-Portrait*, and therefore to be envied in the world of "Scheherazade." Is it available in the randomness of daily life in America? Ashbery has an affectionate eye and an especially affectionate ear for the comic and recalcitrant details of American life: "sloppy joe on bun" stands not too far from the weigela which "does its dusty thing / In fire-hammered air." In "Mixed Feelings" several young girls photographed lounging around a fighter bomber "circa 1942 vintage" summon up a sense of the resistant particulars which tease the imagination. The fading news-shot flirts with the poet's curiosity. He names the girls of that period affectionately—the Ruths and Lindas and Pats and Sheilas. He wants to know their hobbies. "Aw nerts, / One of them might say, this guy's too much for me." Each side has its innings: the girls are imagined as wanting to dump the poet and go off to the garment center for a cup of coffee; the poet, laughing at their "tiny intelligences" for thinking they're in New York, recognizes that their scene is set in California. What's delightful about this poem is the relaxed exchange of imagining mind with imagined objects, a kind of seesaw in which each is given independent play. Though the girls are dismissed, he is fully prepared to encounter them again in some modern airport as "astonishingly young and fresh as when this picture was made."

One of the most engaging things about Ashbery's book is his own susceptibility to American sprawl, while understanding its impossible cost. There is a serious undertone—or is it the main current?—in a poem called "The One Thing That Can Save America."

> The quirky things that happen to me, and I tell you,
> And you instantly know what I mean?

> What remote orchard reached by winding roads
> Hides them? Where are these roots?

Along with a healthy love of quirkiness, Ashbery expresses a bafflement that any individual radiance is ever communicated from one person to another. The "One Thing" that can "Save America" is a very remote and ironic chance that

>   limited
> Steps . . . can be taken against danger
> Now and in the future, in cool yards,
> In quiet small houses in the country,
> Our country, in fenced areas, in cool shady streets.

The poem reaches a political point which it would be oversimplifying, but suggestive, to call "populist."

The enemy, over and over again, is *generality*. The generalizing habit, he tells us in "All and Some," draws us together "at the place of a bare pedestal. / Too many armies, too many dreams, and that's / It." I don't mean that *Self-Portrait in a Convex Mirror* gets down to cracker-barrel preaching. There is too much self-mockery for that.

> Do you remember how we used to gather
> The woodruff, the woodruff? But all things
> Cannot be emblazoned, but surely many
> Can, and those few devoted
> By a caprice beyond the majesty
> Of time's maw live happy useful lives
> Unaware that the universe is a vast incubator.

What I am getting at is that Ashbery's new variety of tone gives him access to many impulses unresolved and frustrated in *The Double Dream of Spring*.

Whitman's invitation for American poets to loaf and invite their souls can't have had many responses more mysterious, peculiar, searching and beautiful than Ashbery's recent poems. Where he will go from here there is, to use one of his titles, "no way of knowing." What *is* important is that Ashbery, who was on speaking terms with both the formalism of the American 1950s and the unbuttoned verse of the 1960s, is now bold and beyond them. His three most recent books have explored apparently contradictory impulses—a melancholy withdrawal and a bewildered, beguiling openness—which stand in provocative tension with one another. Older readers have tended to find the poems "difficult"; younger readers either do not experience that difficulty or see past it, recognizing gestures and a voice that speak directly to them. Perhaps it is reassuring to them: a voice which is honest about its confusions; a voice which lays claim to ravishing visions but doesn't scorn distraction, is in fact prey to it. Ashbery does what all real poets do, and like all innovators his accents seem both too close and too far from the everyday, not quite what we imagine *art* to be. He mystifies and demystifies at once.

A FINAL NOTE

> I don't think my poetry is inaccessible. People say it's
> very private, but I think it's about the privacy of every-
> one.   JOHN ASHBERY[1]

Reading Ashbery's work, I often have the feeling that he speaks
not only to his moment but to the condition of much postmodern-
ist poetry. Not because he makes noble pronouncements about poetry as Wallace Stevens did. Almost the opposite. At random moments at home or on the street, he has an odd radar about just how
much and how little poetry can do for the occasion. His is the
reaction of someone who has stumbled into a place of stress rather
than someone who has deliberately painted himself into a corner
in order to write about frustration. His offhand statement about
privacy is a good example, a kind of optical illusion. It acknowl-
edges the reduced scale of much recent poetry. Looked at again it
stresses the ambitions of someone who concentrates on what is private. Ashbery is not simply reminding us that poetry has access to
the inner life; he is emphasizing the unique power of language to
reveal how much of external life the inner life displaces.

Ashbery's poems, even in their casual way, stand as a penetrating
critique of the autobiographical impulse in recent American poetry. With all his openness to distraction, the way his poems ride
with the moment, still Ashbery seems almost hopeless, almost desperate, about the transmission of that life to the page:

> All diaries are alike, clear and cold, with
> The outlook for continued cold. They are placed

> Horizontal, parallel to the earth,
> Like the unencumbering dead. Just time to reread this
> And the past slips through your fingers, wishing
>   you were there.

This is what "A Man of Words" has to say. Ashbery reminds us how difficult it is to salvage experience. His poems expose an inner environment in which the outer "fact" struggles to find a place. Acting out a failure to turn the present into a usable past, his poems have the uncanny ability to expose, in the everyday, our unadmitted signs of conflict and frustration. Ashbery's work often gives an implied and unexpected twist to Jarrell's remark about the limits of verse:

> If there were only some mechanism . . . for reasonably and systematically converting into poetry what we see and feel and are.

Taking it as a given that there are no such satisfactions, Ashbery stresses the activity of consciousness and not its power to fix or communicate its content. His is an extreme and valuable and melancholy position, fully conveyed in the rhythms and recognitions of this passage from *Three Poems*:

> You see that you cannot do without it, that singular isolated moment that has now already slipped so far into the past that it seems a mere spark. You cannot do without it and you cannot have it. At this point a drowsiness overtakes you as of total fatigue and indifference; in this unnatural, dreamy state the objects you have been contemplating take on a life of their own, in and for themselves. It seems to you that you are eavesdropping and can understand their private language. They are not talking about you at all, but are telling each other curious private stories about things you can only half comprehend, and other things that have a meaning only for themselves and are beyond any kind of understanding. And these in turn would know other sets of objects, limited to their own perceptions and at the limit of the scope of visibility of those that discuss them and dream about them. It could be that time and space are filled up with these to infinity and beyond; that there is no such thing as a void, only

endless lists of things that may or may not be aware of one
another, the "sad variety of woe." And this pointless diversity
plunges you into a numbing despair and blankness. The
whole world seems dyed the same melancholy hue. Nothing
in it can arouse your feelings. Even the sun seems dead. And
all because you succumbed to what seemed an innocent and
perfectly natural craving, to have your cake and eat it too,
forgetting that, widespread as it is, it cannot be excused on
any human grounds because it cannot be realized. Therefore
even to contemplate it is a sin.[2]

A dead end for the ego—but Ashbery's example helps us understand work less apparently random and remorseful than his own.
The new license to write more explicitly about the self has brought
with it in all the poets I have discussed an equal and opposite
awareness of the difficulties of such writing. Among these poets,
only Rich seems impatient with these limitations, refusing to accept them, constantly placing herself at new boundaries to be
crossed. For the others—for Lowell and Merrill in their quite contrary ways—the difficulties of writing about the self have become a
resource, part of their subject. Even a poet like Bishop, whose verse
is so manifestly finished and "objective," turns in her later, openly
autobiographical poems to thinking about the ways in which her
earlier poems try over and over again to lay claim to an interior
landscape. She prompts readers to look for the autobiographical
element not in the poem as "product," not in its content, but in
the energies these poems deploy. "In the Waiting Room" and "In
the Village" help us see how Bishop's earlier poems make environ-
ments which only momentarily displace or refigure enduring feelings of loss.

I had originally planned as subtitle for this book, "Imagination
and Autobiography in Recent American Poetry." Writing about
"five temperaments" is only a start on such a subject, but I wanted
some way of suggesting a historical dimension. All Romantic and
post-Romantic poetry could be considered, if the point were
pressed, "autobiographical." It is the circumstantial and documentary details, the faithfulness to a social surface, that make au-

tobiographical elements more explicit in the poetry of our American contemporaries. But that poetry is still re-enacting the struggles with consciousness which have enriched and bedevilled lyric poetry since Wordsworth. In contemporary poetry it has been interesting to watch, over the curve of a poet's life, over the sustained efforts of several books of verse, the ways a poet will find to transcend or subvert, though never jettison, the autobiographical commitment. Or, to look at it from another angle, we learn from the best of these poets what writing can and cannot do for their lives.

NOTES

Books from which I have cited lines by the five principal poets are identified on pp. 211-12.

INTRODUCTION

1. Helen Vendler, "A Quarter of Poetry," *The New York Times Book Review* (April 6, 1975), p. 4.
2. Randall Jarrell, *Poetry and the Age* (1953; repr. Random House, Vintage, 1959), pp. 160-61.
3. John Ashbery, *Self-Portrait in a Convex Mirror* (Viking, 1975), p. 81.
4. Louis Simpson, *"Divine Comedies,"* *The New York Times Book Review* (March 21, 1976), p. 7.
5. Adrienne Rich, *Diving into the Wreck* (W. W. Norton, 1973), p. 55. A similar critical point is made by Helen Vendler, "Ghostlier Demarcations, Keener Sounds," *Parnassus: Poetry in Review* (Fall/Winter 1973), p. 30.
6. Richard Howard, *Alone with America* (Atheneum, 1969), p. xiii.
7. *The Collected Poems of Frank O'Hara*, ed. Donald Allen (Alfred A. Knopf, 1971), p. ix.
8. Richard Poirier, *A World Elsewhere* (Oxford University Press, 1966), p. 11.
9. *The Craft of Poetry: Interviews from the New York Quarterly*, ed. William Packard (Doubleday, 1974), p. 123.
10. Wallace Stevens, *The Necessary Angel* (1951; repr. Random House, Vintage, 1965), pp. 120-21.

I ELIZABETH BISHOP

1. Randall Jarrell, *Poetry and the Age* (1953; repr. Random House, Vintage, 1959), p. 213.

2. Robert Lowell, "On 'Skunk Hour,'" repr. in *Robert Lowell: A Collection of Critical Essays*, ed. Thomas Parkinson (Prentice-Hall, 1968), p. 133.

3. Stephen Stepanchev, *American Poetry Since 1945* (Harper and Row, 1965), p. 74.

4. Howard Nemerov, *Reflexions on Poetry & Poetics* (Rutgers University Press, 1972), p. 6.

5. Quoted in Anne Stevenson, *Elizabeth Bishop* (Twayne, 1966), p. 66.

6. "In the Village," *Questions of Travel* (Farrar, Straus and Giroux, 1965), pp. 48-49.

7. Ibid., pp. 76-77.

8. *The Collected Poems of Wallace Stevens* (Alfred A. Knopf, 1954), p. 383.

9. Poems in this section are cited from *Geography III* (Farrar, Straus and Giroux, 1976).

II   ROBERT LOWELL

1. "For Elizabeth Bishop 4," *History* (Farrar, Straus and Giroux, 1973), p. 198.

2. "On 'Skunk Hour,'" repr. in *Robert Lowell: A Collection of Critical Essays*, ed. Thomas Parkinson (Prentice-Hall, 1968), p. 132.

3. Ibid., p. 133.

4. *Writers at Work: The Paris Review Interviews—Second Series* (Viking, 1965), p. 347. The interviewer is Frederick Seidel.

5. Ibid., p. 346.

6. "A Conversation with Robert Lowell," *Modern Occasions* (Winter 1972), p. 45.

7. M. L. Rosenthal, "Robert Lowell and the Poetry of Confession," repr. in *Critical Essays*, ed. Parkinson, p. 114.

8. *Modern Occasions*, p. 44.

9. Ibid., p. 32.

10. Ibid., pp. 31-32.

11. *Notebook 1967-68* (Farrar, Straus and Giroux, 1969), p. 159.

12. *History*, p. 7.

13. *Modern Occasions*, p. 44.

14. *Writers at Work*, p. 348.

15. Patrick Cosgrave, *The Public Poetry of Robert Lowell* (Taplinger, 1972), p. 24.

16. Richard Poirier, "Our Truest Historian," *Book Week* (October 11, 1964), p. 1.

17. Irvin Ehrenpreis, "The Age of Lowell," repr. in *Critical Essays*, ed. Parkinson, p. 89.

18. "On 'Skunk Hour,' " p. 133.

19. Ibid., p. 131.

20. John Berryman, "Despondency and Madness," repr. in *Critical Essays*, ed. Parkinson, p. 126.

21. Gabriel Pearson, "Lowell's Marble Meanings," *The Survival of Poetry*, ed. Martin Dodsworth (Faber and Faber, London, 1970), p. 91.

22. Ibid., p. 92.

23. Stephen Yenser, *Circle to Circle* (University of California Press, 1975), p. 121.

24. Ibid., p. 136.

25. Ibid., p. 215.

26. *History*, p. 140.

27. *Book Week*, p. 16.

28. *Notebook* (rev. ed., 1970), p. 263.

29. *Modern Occasions*, p. 30.

30. See Yenser, pp. 273-97 and Alan Williamson, *Pity the Monsters* (Yale University Press, 1974), pp. 156-215.

31. Randall Jarrell, *Poetry and the Age* (1953; repr. Random House, Vintage, 1959), p. 193.

32. Yenser, p. 306.

33. Ibid., p. 311.

III   JAMES MERRILL

1. "An Interview with James Merrill," *Contemporary Literature* IX (Winter 1968), p. 5. The interviewer is Donald Sheehan.

2. "The Poet: Private," *Saturday Review/The Arts* (December 2, 1972), p. 45. The interviewer is David Kalstone.

3. *Contemporary Literature*, p. 8.

4. Marcel Proust, *Remembrance of Things Past* (*Time Regained*, tr. Stephen Hudson: Chatto & Windus, 1931), XII, 218.

5. "An Interview with James Merrill," *Shenandoah* XIX (Summer 1968), p. 9. The interviewer is Ashley Brown.

6. Letter to David Kalstone, n.d.

7. *Saturday Review*, p. 45.

8. To *Nights and Days*, *Braving the Elements* and *Divine Comedies*, respectively.

9. Richard Saez, "James Merrill's Oedipal Fire," *Parnassus: Poetry in Review* (Fall/Winter 1974), p. 172.

10. Ibid., pp. 179-81.

11. Richard Poirier, *A World Elsewhere* (Oxford University Press, 1966), p. 19.

12. I am indebted for this point to Alan Nadel.

13. Marcel Proust, *Remembrance of Things Past* (*The Past Recaptured*, tr. Frederick Blossom, Random House, 1932), II, 1017.

IV   ADRIENNE RICH

1. "When We Dead Awaken: Writing as Revision," repr. in *Adrienne Rich's Poetry*, eds. Barbara Charlesworth Gelpi and Albert Gelpi (W. W. Norton, 1975), p. 97.

2. Thomas Edwards, *Imagination and Power* (Oxford University Press, 1971), pp. 220, 225.

3. Albert Gelpi, "Adrienne Rich: The Poetics of Change," repr. in *Adrienne Rich's Poetry*, p. 145.

4. "When We Dead Awaken," p. 94.

5. Ibid.

6. Helen Vendler, "Ghostlier Demarcations, Keener Sounds," *Parnassus: Poetry in Review* (Fall/Winter 1973), p. 18.

7. "When We Dead Awaken," pp. 95-96.

8. *Poems: Selected and New, 1950-1974* (W. W. Norton, 1975), p. 248.

9. *Of Woman Born* (W. W. Norton, 1976), jacket copy.

10. *Parnassus*, p. 30.

V   JOHN ASHBERY

1. John Ashbery and David Kermani, "Taking Care of the Luxuries (The Shiraz Festival)," *Saturday Review/The Arts*, November 4, 1972, pp. 60-63.

2. Louis A. Osti, "The Craft of John Ashbery: an Interview," *Confrontation* 9 (Fall 1974), p. 89.

3. *The Guardian* (April 19, 1975), p. 8.

4. *The Craft of Poetry: Interviews from the New York Quarterly*, ed. William Packard (Doubleday, 1974), p. 124.

5. *Confrontation*, p. 94.

6. *Craft of Poetry*, p. 130.

7. Ibid., p. 126.

8. *Confrontation*, p. 87.
9. *Craft of Poetry*, p. 119.
10. Ibid., p. 126.
11. Ibid., p. 121.

A FINAL NOTE

1. Interview by Anna Quindlen, *The New York Post* (February 7, 1976).
2. John Ashbery, *Three Poems* (1972), pp. 84-85.

CREDITS

Lines of poetry by the following poets are taken from the indicated volumes:

By Elizabeth Bishop. Reprinted with the permission of Farrar, Straus and Giroux, Inc. From *The Complete Poems*, copyright © 1938, 1939, 1947, 1948, 1949, 1955, 1956, 1959, 1962 by Elizabeth Bishop, copyright renewed © 1974, 1975, 1976 by Elizabeth Bishop. "At the Fishhouses" appeared originally in *The New Yorker*. From *Questions of Travel* by Elizabeth Bishop, copyright © 1953, 1965 by Elizabeth Bishop. "In the Village" appeared originally in *The New Yorker*. From *Geography III* by Elizabeth Bishop, copyright © 1971, 1972, 1976 by Elizabeth Bishop. All of these poems appeared originally in *The New Yorker*.

By Robert Lowell. Reprinted with the permission of Farrar, Straus and Giroux, Inc. From *Life Studies*, copyright © 1956, 1959 by Robert Lowell. From *History* by Robert Lowell, copyright © 1967, 1968, 1969, 1970, 1973 by Robert Lowell. From *The Union Dead* by Robert Lowell, copyright © 1956, 1959, 1961, 1962, 1963, 1964 by Robert Lowell.

By James Merrill, from *First Poems*, copyright © 1951 James Merrill, published by Alfred A. Knopf, New York, 1951; from *The Country of a Thousand Years of Peace*, copyright © 1958 James Merrill, published by Alfred A. Knopf, New York, 1959, rev. ed. published by Atheneum, New York, 1970; *Water Street*, copyright © 1962 James

Merrill, published by Atheneum, New York, 1962; *Nights and Days*, copyright © 1966 James Merrill, published by Atheneum, New York, 1966; *The Fire Screen*, copyright © 1969 James Merrill, published by Atheneum, New York, 1969; *Braving the Elements*, copyright © 1972 James Merrill, published by Atheneum, New York, 1972; *Divine Comedies*, copyright © 1976 James Merrill, published by Atheneum, New York, 1976.

By Adrienne Rich, from *Poems: Selected and New, 1950-1974*, copyright © 1975 Adrienne Rich, published by W. W. Norton & Co., Inc., New York, 1975; and from "Cartographies of Silence," *Field* (October 1975).

By John Ashbery, from *Some Trees*, copyright © 1956 John Ashbery, published by the Yale University Press, New Haven, Conn., 1956; from *Rivers and Mountains* copyright © 1966 John Ashbery, published by Holt, Rinehart & Winston, New York, 1966; from *The Double Dream of Spring*, copyright © 1970 John Ashbery, published by E. P. Dutton & Co., Inc., New York, 1970; from *Three Poems*, copyright © 1972 John Ashbery, published by The Viking Press, Inc., New York, 1972; from *Self-Portrait in a Convex Mirror*, copyright © 1975 John Ashbery, published by The Viking Press, Inc., New York, 1975; from *Houseboat Days*, copyright © 1977 John Ashbery, published by The Viking Press, Inc., New York, 1977.